The Kids' Guide to Birds of Texas

Fun Facts, Activities and 90 Cool Birds

T0126051

by Stan Tekiela

Adventure Publications
Cambridge, Minnesota

DEDICATION

To all the children who enjoy the world of birds as much as I do.

ACKNOWLEDGMENTS

Special thanks to the National Wildlife Refuge System along with state and local agencies, both public and private, for stewarding the lands that are critical to the many bird species we so love.

Edited by Dan Downing, Sandy Livoti, and Brett Ortler
Cover and book design by Jonathan Norberg
Illustrations by Elleyna Ruud
Range maps produced by Anthony Hertzel

Cover photos by Stan Tekiela. Front: Golden-fronted Woodpecker, Vermilion Flycatcher, Crested Caracara, Painted Bunting, American Goldfinch, Mountain Bluebird **Back:** Great-horned Owl

All photos by Stan Tekiela except pg. 140 (juvenile) by **Albert Barr/Shutterstock;** pg. 142 (cap) by **Steve Byland/Shutterstock.com;** pp. 110 (wings), 126 (juvenile) and 172 (wings) by **Dudley Edmondson;** pg. 208 (feet) by **Phil Friar/Shutterstock.com;** pg. 169 by **Dennis Jacobsen/Shutterstock.com;** 202 (winter) by **Kevin T. Karlson;** pg. 97 by **Maslowski Wildlife Productions;** pg. 228 by **Dr. Pixel/Shutterstock.com;** pg. 162 (wings) by **Hartmut Walter;** pg. 38 (juvenile) by **Brian K. Wheeler;** and pg. 96 (side) by **Jim Zipp**

To the best of the publisher's knowledge, all photos were of live birds. Some were photographed in a controlled condition.

10 9 8 7 6 5 4 3

The Kids' Guide to Birds of Texas: Fun Facts, Activities and 90 Cool Birds
Copyright © 2020 by Stan Tekiela
Published by Adventure Publications
An imprint of AdventureKEEN
310 Garfield Street South
Cambridge, Minnesota 55008
(800) 678-7006
www.adventurepublications.net
All rights reserved
Printed in China
ISBN 978-1-59193-965-8 (pbk.); ISBN 978-1-59193-966-5 (ebook)

Quick-Flip Color Guide

TABLE OF CONTENTS

Introduction

The Birds

Bird Food Fun for the Family

More Activities for the Bird-Minded

COOL BIRDS IN TEXAS

The Kids' Guide to Birds of Texas is a fun, easy-to-use guide for anyone interested in seeing and identifying birds. As a child, I spent hours of enjoyment watching birds come to a wooden feeder that my father built in our backyard. We were the only family in the neighborhood who fed birds, and we became known as the nature family.

Now, more people feed birds in their backyards than those who go hunting or fishing combined. Not only has it become very popular to feed and watch birds, but young and old alike are also identifying them and learning more about them.

Texas is a fantastic place to see all sorts of birds. In fact, more than 600 species are found here! That makes it one of the top states to watch an incredible variety of birds. In this field guide for Texas, I'm featuring 90 of the most common of these great species.

We have marvelous habitats in Texas that are perfect for birds. Each **habitat** supports different kinds of birds. The southeast part of the state sits on the Gulf of Mexico. Beaches and rocky shores are wonderful places to see a wide variety of shorebirds, such as Brown Pelicans, and wading birds, such as Snowy Egrets. Texas also has pine woodlands, which are home to many smaller songbirds, like White-breasted Nuthatches.

Texas has lots of **oak savanna** forest habitats! Birds that prefer this habitat are often bright and colorful, and they build nests in leafy trees.

In addition, we have a lot of ponds, rivers and lakes. These freshwater environments are home to Ring-necked Ducks, Roseate Spoonbills, Great Blue Herons, White Ibis and more.

The weather here also plays a role in the kinds of birds we see. Carolina Wrens, Vermilion Flycatchers and many more birds nest here during summer. Migrating shorebirds, such as American Avocets and Killdeer, come to Texas for our warm winters. A wide array of other birds, including Sandhill Cranes and Bald Eagles, live here all year long. On top of that, backyard birds, most notably buntings, bluebirds and cardinals, enjoy our seasons year-round.

As you can see, Texas is a terrific place to watch all kinds of cool birds. It is my sincere hope that you and your family will like watching and feeding birds as much as I did with my family when I was a kid. Let this handy book guide you into a lifetime of appreciating birds and nature.

BODY BASICS OF A BIRD

It's good to know the names of a bird's body parts. The right terminology will help you describe and identify a bird when you talk about it with your friends and family.

The basic parts of a bird are labeled in the illustration below. This drawing is a combination (composite) of several birds and should not be regarded as one particular species.

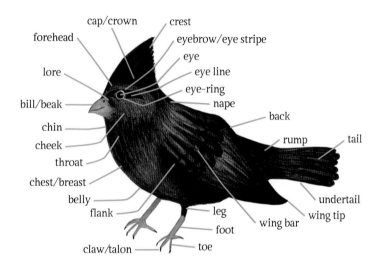

AMAZING NESTS

I am fascinated with bird nests! They are amazing structures that do more than just provide a place for egg laying. Nests create a small climate-controlled environment that's beneficial for both keeping the eggs warm and raising the young after they hatch.

From the high treetops to the ground, there are many kinds of nests. Some are simple, while others are complex. In any case, they function in nearly the same way. Nests help to contain the eggs so they don't roll away. They also help to keep baby birds warm on cold nights, cool on hot days and dry during rains.

The following illustrations show the major types of nests that birds build in Texas.

GROUND **PLATFORM** **CUP** **PENDULOUS** **CAVITY**

A **ground nest** can be a mound of plant materials on the ground or in the water. Some are just a shallow spot scraped in the earth.

A **platform nest** is a cluster of sticks with a depression in the center. It is secured to the platform of a tree fork or to several tree branches.

A **cup nest** has a cupped interior, like a bowl.

A **pendulous nest** is a woven nest that hangs and swings freely, like a pendulum, from a branch.

A **cavity nest** is simply a cavity, or hole, usually in a tree.

The first step in nest building is to choose an appropriate site. Each bird species has a unique requirement for this. Some birds, such as American Robins, just need a tree branch. Others, like Eastern Bluebirds, look for a cavity and build the nest inside. Still others, such as Killdeer, search for camouflaged ground to scrape out a nest. Sometimes birds such as Turkey Vultures don't bother building a nest at all if they spot a hard-to-reach cliff or rocky ledge, where it will be safe to lay their eggs.

Nest materials usually consist of common natural items found in the area, like sticks or dried grass. Birds use other materials, such as mud or spiderwebs, to glue the materials together.

One of the amazing things about nest construction is that the parents don't need building plans or tool belts. They already know by instinct how to build nests, and they use their beaks and feet as their main tools.

To bring in nesting materials, birds must make many trips back and forth to the nest site. Most use their beaks to hold as much material as possible during each trip. Some of the bigger birds, like Ospreys, use larger materials, such as thick sticks and thin branches. They grasp and carry these items with their feet.

Nest building can take two to four days or longer, depending on the species and nest type. The simpler the nest, the faster the construction. Mourning Dove parents, for example, take just a few days to collect one to two dozen sticks for their platform nest. Woodpecker pairs, however, work upwards of a week to **excavate**, or dig out, a suitable nesting cavity. Large and more complicated platform nests, such as a Bald Eagle nest, may take weeks or even a month to complete, but these can be used for years and are worth the extra effort.

WHO BUILT THAT NEST?

In the majority of bird species, the chief builder is the female. In other species, both the female and the male typically share in the construction equally.

In general, when male and female birds look vastly different, the female does most of the work. When the male and female look alike or appear very similar, they tend to share the tasks of nest building and feeding the young. Alternatively, some species of woodpeckers have a different building plan. When they chisel out a nesting chamber, often the male does more of the work after the female has chosen the site.

ATTRACTING BIRDS WITH FEEDERS

To get more birds to visit your yard, an easy way to invite them is to put out bird feeders. Bird feeders are often as unique as the birds themselves, so the types of feeders you use really depends on the kinds of birds you're trying to attract.

HOPPER   **TUBE**   **GROUND**   **SUET**   **NECTAR**   **MEALWORM**

Hopper feeders are often wooden or plastic. Designed to hold a large amount of seeds, they often have a slender opening along the bottom, which dispenses the seeds. Birds land along the sides and help themselves to the food. Hopper feeders work well as main feeders in conjunction with other types of feeders. They are perfect for offering several kinds of seed mixes for cardinals, finches, nuthatches, chickadees and more.

Tube feeders with large seed ports and multiple perches are very popular. Often mostly plastic, they tend to be rugged enough to last several years and can be easily cleaned. These feeders are great for black oil sunflower seeds and seed mixes, which are favorites of cardinals and all the other bird species that also visit hopper feeders.

Some tube feeders have small holes, allowing incredibly tiny thistle seeds to be dispensed just a few at a time. Use this kind of feeder to offer Nyjer seed, which will attract various finches.

Other styles of tube feeders have a wire mesh covering with openings large enough for birds to extract one of their favorite foods—peanuts out of the shell. Most birds enjoy peanuts, so these feeders will be some of the most popular in your yard. Another variety of tube feeder has openings large enough for peanuts in the shell. These are also very popular with the birds.

Ground feeders allow a wide variety of birds to access the food. The simplest and easiest feeders to use, they consist of a flat platform with a lip around the edges to keep seeds and corn from spilling out. Some have a roof to keep rain and snow off the food. With or without a roof, drainage holes in the bottom are important. Ground feeders will bring in towhees and many other birds to your backyard, including doves, and even mallards if you're near water.

Suet feeders are simply wire cages that hold cakes of **suet**. The wire allows woodpeckers, nuthatches and other birds to cling securely to the feeder while pecking out chunks of suet. The best suet feeders have a vertical extension at the bottom where a woodpecker can brace its tail and support itself while feeding. These are called tail-prop suet feeders.

Nectar feeders are glass or plastic containers that hold sugar water. These feeders usually have plastic parts that are bright red, a color that is extremely attractive to hummingbirds, but orioles and woodpeckers will also stop for a drink. They often have up to four ports for access to the liquid and yellow bee guards to prevent bees from getting inside.

Mealworm feeders can be very basic—a simple glass or plastic cup or container will do. Pick one with sides tall enough and make sure the material is slippery enough to stop the lively mealworms from crawling out. Bluebirds especially love this wiggly treat!

HOW TO USE THIS GUIDE

Birds move pretty fast, so you don't often get a lot of time to observe them. To help you quickly find the birds in the book, this guide is organized by color. Simply note the most prominent color of the bird you've seen. A Pileated Woodpecker, for example, is black and white and has a red crest. Since this bird is mostly black and white, you would find it in the black and white section.

Within each color section, the birds are organized by size, from small to large. Use the Real Quick sidebar to find the size that your bird appears to be.

When the male and female of a species are different colors (like the Northern Shoveler pair below), they are shown in their own color sections. In these cases, the opposite sex is included in an inset photo with a page reference so you can easily turn to it.

If you already know the name of the bird you've seen, use the checklist/index to get the page number, and flip to it to learn more about the bird.

To further help you with identification, check the range maps to see where and when the bird you have sighted is normally in Texas. Range maps capture our current knowledge of where the birds are during a given year (presence) but do not indicate how many birds are in the area (density). In addition, since birds fly around freely, it's possible to see them outside of their ranges. So please use the maps to get a general idea of where the birds are most likely to be seen.

For more about the information given for each bird in this guide, turn to the Northern Cardinal sample on pp. 16–17.

While you're learning about birds and identifying them, don't forget to check out the fun-filled things to do starting on pg. 220. Score a big hit with the birds in your yard by creating tasty treats or making your own bird food from the recipes. Put out some nesting materials to help birds build their nests. Consider signing up for a cool citizen science project suitable for the entire family. These are just a few of the activities that are such great fun, you'll want to do them all!

Northern Cardinal

Common name

Look for the black mask

Field markings that help identify the bird

MALE

Colored border shows
the color section of
the opposite sex

Turn to the page number to see
the opposite sex of the species

FEMALE
pg. 93

What to look for:
outstanding features; may include other plumages and descriptions

Length from head to tail

Size
8-9"

Where you'll find them:
where you're most likely to see the bird

Calls and songs:
songs, calls and other sounds the bird makes

Type of nest the bird calls home

Nest
CUP

On the move:
anything about flight, flocks, travel and other movements

Type of feeder the bird generally visits

Feeder
HOPPER

What they eat:
foods the bird eats and the kinds of feeders it visits

Range map

Nest:
type of nest; may include nest site, materials and more

The bold word means it is defined in the glossary

year-round
summer
migration
winter

Eggs, chicks and childcare:
number of eggs, color and marks; **incubation** and feeding duties; may include how many broods

Spends the winter:
where the bird goes when it's cold or when food is scarce

After you've seen it, checkmark it

SAW ✓ IT!

STAN'S COOL STUFF

Fun and interesting facts about the bird. Information not typically found in other field guides.

Brown-headed Cowbird

Look for the brown head

MALE

FEMALE
pg.89

What to look for:
glossy black bird with a chocolate-brown head and a sharp, pointed gray bill

Where you'll find them:
forest edges, open fields, farmlands and backyards

Calls and songs:
sings a low, gurgling song that sounds like water moving; cowbird young are raised by other bird parents, but they still end up singing and calling like their own parents, whom they've never heard

On the move:
Mom flies quietly to another bird's nest, swiftly lays an egg, then flies quickly away

What they eat:
insects and seeds; visits seed feeders

Nest:
doesn't nest; lays eggs in the nests of other birds

Eggs, chicks and childcare:
white eggs with brown marks; the **host** bird incubates any number of cowbird eggs in her nest and feeds the cowbird young along with her own

Spends the winter:
in Texas and other southern states

REAL QUICK

Size
7½"

Nest
NONE

Feeder
TUBE OR HOPPER

year-round

SAW ✓ **IT!**

19

European Starling

Look for the glittering, iridescent feathers

BREEDING

WINTER

What to look for:
shiny and **iridescent** purplish-black in spring and summer, speckled in fall and winter; yellow bill in spring, gray in fall; pointed wings and a short tail

Where you'll find them:
lines up with other starlings on power lines; found in all habitats but usually associated with people, farms, suburban yards and cities

Calls and songs:
mimics the songs of up to 20 bird species; mimics other sounds, even imitating the human voice

On the move:
large family groups gather with blackbirds in fall

What they eat:
bugs, seeds and fruit; visits seed and **suet** feeders

Nest:
cavity; filled with dried grass; often takes a cavity from other birds

Eggs, chicks and childcare:
4–6 bluish eggs with brown marks; Mom and Dad sit on the eggs and feed the babies

Spends the winter:
in Texas and other southern states

REAL QUICK

Size
7½"

Nest
CAVITY

Feeder
TUBE OR HOPPER

year-round

SAW IT!

STAN'S COOL STUFF

The starling is a mimic that can sound like any other bird. It's not a native bird; 100 starlings from Europe were introduced to New York City in 1890–91. Today, European Starlings are one of the most common songbirds in the country.

Eastern & Spotted Towhee

Look for the black head

EASTERN MALE

FEMALE
pg. 97

SPOTTED MALE

FEMALE
pg. 97

What to look for:
mostly black bird with rusty sides, a white belly, red eyes, and a long black tail with a white tip

Where to find them:
shrubby areas with short trees and thick bushes, backyards and parks

Calls and songs:
calls "tow-hee" distinctly; also has a characteristic **call** that sounds like "drink-your-tea"

On the move:
short flights between shrubby areas and heavy **cover**; flashes white wing patches during flight

What they eat:
insects, seeds and fruit; comes to ground feeders

Nest:
cup; Mom constructs the nest

Eggs, chicks and childcare:
3–4 creamy-white eggs with brown marks; Mom incubates the eggs; Dad and Mom feed the young

Spends the winter:
in Texas and other southern states

REAL QUICK

Size
8½"

Nest
CUP

Feeder
GROUND

Eastern

Spotted

year-round
winter

SAW IT!

STAN'S COOL STUFF

The towhee is named for its distinctive "tow-hee" call. It hops backward with both feet, raking leaves to find insects and seeds. It is a large species of sparrow, nearly the size of a robin. It often has more than one clutch of eggs each breeding season.

Red-winged Blackbird

Look for the red-and-yellow shoulder patches

MALE

FEMALE
pg. 99

What to look for:
black bird with red-and-yellow shoulder patches on upper wings; shoulder patches can be partially or completely covered up

Where you'll find them:
around marshes, wetlands, lakes and rivers

Calls and songs:
male sings and repeats calls from cattail tops and the surrounding **vegetation**

On the move:
flocks with as many as 10,000 birds gather in autumn, often with other blackbirds

What they eat:
seeds in spring and autumn, insects in summer; visits seed and **suet** feeders

Nest:
cup; in a thick stand of cattails over shallow water

Eggs, chicks and childcare:
3–4 speckled bluish-green eggs; Mom does all the incubating, but both parents feed the babies

Spends the winter:
in Texas and other southern states, Mexico and Central America

REAL QUICK

Size
8½"

Nest
CUP

Feeder
TUBE OR HOPPER

year-round

SAW IT!

STAN'S COOL STUFF

During autumn and winter, thousands of these birds gather in farm fields, wetlands and marshes. Come spring, males sing to defend territories and show off their wing patches (**epaulets**) to the females. Later, males can be aggressive when defending their nests.

25

Common Grackle

Look for the shiny bluish-black head

What to look for:
shiny bluish-black **iridescent** head, a purplish-brown body and super-bright golden eyes

Where you'll find them:
evergreen trees and shrubs, suburban and urban yards, open fields

Calls and songs:
gives a loud, raspy **call**

On the move:
travels in large flocks with other blackbirds; flight is usually level as opposed to an up-and-down pattern; male holds his tail in a deep V shape

What they eat:
fruit, seeds and bugs; visits seed and **suet** feeders

Nest:
cup; usually in a **colony** of up to 75 mated pairs

Eggs, chicks and childcare:
4–5 speckled greenish-white eggs; Mom sits on the eggs; Mom and Dad give food to the babies

Spends the winter:
in Texas and other southern states; moves around to find food

REAL QUICK

Size
11–13"

Nest
CUP

Feeder
HOPPER

year-round
winter

SAW IT!

STAN'S COOL STUFF

The Common Grackle is a member of the blackbird family. Unlike most birds, it has stronger muscles to open its mouth. The muscles help it to pry apart crevices, where it finds bugs to eat. It's kind of like playing hide-and-seek for its food.

American Coot

Look for the white bill

What to look for:
gray-to-black with a duck-like white bill, red eyes

Where you'll find them:
in large flocks on open water

Calls and songs:
a unique series of creaks, groans and clicks

On the move:
bobs head while swimming; takes off from water by scrambling across it with wings flapping; huge flocks of up to 1,000 birds gather for migration; migrates at night

What they eat:
insects and aquatic plants

Nest:
ground nest floating in water, anchored to plants

Eggs, chicks and childcare:
9–12 speckled pinkish-tan eggs; Mom and Dad sit on the eggs and feed the **hatchlings**

Spends the winter:
in Texas and other southern states, Mexico and Central America

REAL QUICK

Size
13–16"

Nest
GROUND

Feeder
NONE

year-round

SAW IT!

STAN'S COOL STUFF

The coot is not a duck. Instead of webbed feet, it has large lobed toes! It's smaller than most other **waterfowl**, and it is a great diver and swimmer. You probably won't see it flying, but you may spot one trying to escape from a Bald Eagle (pg. 63). It's also called Mud Hen.

Great-tailed Grackle

Look for the long tail

FEMALE
pg. 109

What to look for:
a big all-black bird with a shiny purple sheen on the head and back; really long tail; bright yellow eyes

Where you'll find them:
open areas, backyards, parks

Calls and songs:
high-pitched, vibrating call given over and over

On the move:
seen around parking lots, sitting in trees, walking on the ground, often calling and chasing each other

What they eat:
insects, fruit, seeds; comes to seed feeders

Nest:
cup; Mom builds it

Eggs, chicks and childcare:
3–5 greenish blue eggs with brown markings; Mom incubates and feeds the young

Spends the winter:
stays in Texas all year; moves around to find food

REAL QUICK

Size
17–19"

Nest
CUP

Feeder
HOPPER

year-round

SAW IT!

STAN'S COOL STUFF

Male Great-tailed Grackles make a number of different calls, and they aren't shy about yelling at animals (or people!) who get too close. Very intelligent birds, Great-tailed Grackles are often seen around food trucks, where they might find food scraps.

American Crow

Look for the glossy black feathers

What to look for:
glossy black all over and a black bill

Where you'll find them:
all habitats—wilderness, rural, suburban, cities

Calls and songs:
a harsh "caw" **call**; imitates other birds and people

On the move:
flaps constantly and glides downward; moves around to find food; gathers in huge communal flocks of more than 10,000 birds during winter

What they eat:
fruit, insects, mammals, fish and dead carcasses (**carrion**); visits seed and **suet** feeders

Nest:
platform; adds bright or shiny items and often uses the same site every year if a Great Horned Owl (pg. 133) hasn't taken it

Eggs, chicks and childcare:
4–6 speckled bluish-to-olive eggs; Mom sits on the eggs; Mom and Dad feed the youngsters

Spends the winter:
in Texas

REAL QUICK

Size
18"

Nest
PLATFORM

Feeder
HOPPER

year-round

SAW IT!

STAN'S COOL STUFF

The crow is one of the smartest of all birds. It's very social and often entertains itself by chasing other birds. It eats roadkill but avoids being hit by vehicles. Some can live as long as 20 years! Crows without mates, called helpers, help to raise the young.

Common Raven

Look for the large thick bill

What to look for:
black with a shaggy beard of feathers on throat and chin; long feathers on legs make it look like it's wearing pants

Where you'll find them:
remote or wilderness settings and also cities

Calls and songs:
a deep, raspy call that's lower-pitched than a crow's call; has more pops and unusual calls than a crow

On the move:
known for its aerial acrobatics and long swooping dives; able to soar on thermals

What they eat:
insects, fruit, small animals and dead carcasses (**carrion**), especially roadkill

Nest:
platform; Mom and Dad build at the same site for many years

Eggs, chicks and childcare:
4–6 pale green eggs with brown marks; Mom incubates while Dad brings food

Spends the winter:
in Texas; doesn't move around as much as crows

STAN'S COOL STUFF

The Common Raven may be the smartest bird. When ravens find food, they help out other ravens by telling other ravens where to find it. Ravens build a large nest out of sticks; some nests can be several feet wide!

Black Vulture

Look for the naked dark-gray head

What to look for:
naked dark gray head and legs, an ivory bill and a short tail; appears black in flight with light-gray wing tips

Where you'll find them:
in trees, sunning itself with wings outstretched, drying after a rain

Calls and songs:
mostly **mute**, just grunts and groans

On the move:
holds wings straight out to the sides during flight

What they eat:
dead carcasses (**carrion**); may capture small live mammals; parents **regurgitate** food for the young

Nest:
no nest, or on a stump or the ground; may use an empty nest; often nests with other Black Vultures

Eggs, chicks and childcare:
1–3 light green eggs with dark marks; Mom and Dad do the **incubation** and feed the babies

Spends the winter:
doesn't **migrate**; stays in Texas year-round

REAL QUICK

Size
25-28"

Nest
NONE

Feeder
NONE

year-round

SAW IT!

STAN'S COOL STUFF

People also call this bird the Black Buzzard. It's not as good at finding carrion as the Turkey Vulture (pg. 39), so its sense of smell may be weaker. If startled, especially at the nest, it regurgitates with power and accuracy. Families stay together for up to several years.

Turkey Vulture

Look for the naked red head

JUVENILE

What to look for:
naked red head and legs and an ivory bill; **juvenile** has a gray-to-blackish head and bill

Where you'll find them:
in trees, sunning itself with wings outstretched; drying after a rain

Calls and songs:
mostly **mute**, just grunts and groans

On the move:
holds wings in an upright V in flight, teetering from wing tip to wing tip as it soars and hovers

What they eat:
dead carcasses (**carrion**); parents **regurgitate** food for their young

Nest:
no nest, or in a minimal nest on a cliff, in a cave, or even sometimes in a hollow tree trunk

Eggs, chicks and childcare:
1–3 white eggs with brown marks; Mom and Dad incubate the eggs and feed the baby vultures

Spends the winter:
in Texas, other southern states, Mexico, Central and South America

REAL QUICK

Size
26–32"

Nest
NONE

Feeder
NONE

year-round
summer

SAW IT!

STAN'S COOL STUFF

This is one of the few birds with a good sense of smell. It has a strong bill for tearing apart flesh. Unlike hawks and eagles, it has weak feet more suited for walking than grasping wiggly **prey**. The bare head reduces its risk of getting diseases from carcasses.

Double-crested Cormorant

Look for the large, hooked bill

DRYING OUT

CRESTS

What to look for:
large black waterbird with unusual blue eyes, a long snake-like neck, and large gray bill with a yellow base and hooked tip

Where you'll find them:
usually roosts in large groups in trees near water

Calls and songs:
grunts, pops and groans—none are pleasant sounds at all!

On the move:
swims underwater to catch fish, holding its wings at its sides; flies in a large V-shaped formation

What they eat:
small fish and aquatic insects

Nest:
platform; near or over open water, in a **colony**

Eggs, chicks and childcare:
3–4 bluish-white eggs; parents take turns sitting on the eggs and feeding the young

Spends the winter:
in Texas and other southern states, and Mexico

REAL QUICK

Size
31-35"

Nest
PLATFORM

Feeder
NONE

year-round
migration
winter

SAW IT!

STAN'S COOL STUFF

This bird's outer feathers are different from its inner ones; the outer feathers soak up water, but its body feathers don't. It opens its wings and uses the sun and wind to dry out. "Double-crested" refers to the two unusual crests on its head, but these aren't often seen.

41

Downy Woodpecker

Look for the small, short bill

MALE

FEMALE

What to look for:

spotted wings, white belly, red mark on the back of the head and a small, short bill; female lacks a red mark on the head

Where you'll find them:

wherever trees are present

Calls and songs:

repeats a high-pitched "peek-peek" **call**; drums on trees or logs with its bill to announce its territory

On the move:

flies in an up-and-down pattern; makes short flights from tree to tree

What they eat:

insects and seeds; visits **suet** and seed feeders

Nest:

cavity in a dead tree; digs out a perfectly round entrance hole; the bottom of the cavity is wider than the top, and it's lined with fallen woodchips

Eggs, chicks and childcare:

3–5 white eggs; Mom incubates the eggs; both parents take care of the kiddies

Spends the winter:

doesn't **migrate**; stays in Texas year-round

Nest
CAVITY

Feeder
SUET

year-round

SAW ✓ **IT!**

STAN'S COOL STUFF

The Downy is abundant and widespread where trees are present. Like other woodpeckers, it pulls insects from tiny places with its long, barbed tongue. It has stiff tail feathers, which help to support it as it clings to trees. During winter, it will roost in a cavity.

Hairy Woodpecker

Look for the large bill

MALE

FEMALE

What to look for:
spotted wings, white belly, large bill and red mark on the back of the head; female lacks a red mark

Where you'll find them:
forests and wooded backyards, parks

Calls and songs:
a sharp chirp before landing on feeders; drums on hollow logs, branches or stovepipes in spring

On the move:
short up-and-down flights from tree to tree with rapid wingbeats

What they eat:
insects, nuts, seeds; visits **suet** and seed feeders

Nest:
cavity; prefers a live tree; excavates a larger, more oval entry than the round hole of the Downy Woodpecker (pg. 43); usually excavates under a branch, which helps to shield the entrance

Eggs, chicks and childcare:
3–6 white eggs; parents sit on the eggs and bring food to feed their babies

Spends the winter:
doesn't **migrate**; stays in Texas year-round

REAL QUICK

Size
9"

Nest
CAVITY

Feeder
SUET

year-round

SAW IT!

STAN'S COOL STUFF

The Hairy is nearly identical to the Downy Woodpecker, but it's larger and has a bigger, longer bill. It has a barbed tongue, which it uses to pull out bugs from trees. At the base of its bill, tiny bristle-like feathers protect its nostrils from excavated wood dust.

Red-bellied Woodpecker

Look for the black-and-white striped back

MALE

FEMALE

What to look for:
zebra-striped back, white rump, red crown and red **nape** of neck; female has a light gray crown

Where you'll find them:
shady woodlands, forest edges and backyards

Calls and songs:
calls a loud "querrr" and a low "chug-chug-chug"

On the move:
rapid wingbeats in flight, going up and down like a roller coaster

What they eat:
beetles and other insects, spiders and centipedes, nuts and fruit; visits **suet** and seed feeders

Nest:
cavity in a dead tree; excavates a new hole in last year's tree below the previous cavity

Eggs, chicks and childcare:
4–5 white eggs; Mom and Dad incubate eggs during the day and Dad takes the night duty; both parents feed the baby woodpeckers

Spends the winter:
doesn't **migrate**; stays in Texas year-round and moves around to find food

STAN'S COOL STUFF

This bird is named for its faint pink belly patch. It excavates dead wood to find bugs to eat, and hammers acorns and berries into cracks in trees to store for winter food. Its population and range are increasing across the country.

Golden-fronted Woodpecker

Look for the yellow patch

MALE

FEMALE

What to look for:
black and white zebra-like back; gray head, red crown and a yellow-to-orange back of the neck; yellow patch at base of the upper bill

Where you'll find them:
forests and woods

Calls and songs:
loud "querrr," similar to Red-bellied Woodpecker

On the move:
short up and down, roller coaster-like flight from tree to tree

What they eat:
insects, nuts, seeds, berries; comes to seed and suet feeders

Nest:
cavity that Mom and Dad excavate

Eggs, chicks and childcare:
4–7 white to cream eggs without markings; Mom and Dad incubate eggs during the day and Dad takes the night duty; both parents feed the baby woodpeckers

Spends the winter:
in Texas; moves around to find food

REAL QUICK

Size
9½"

Nest
CAVITY

Feeder
TUBE OR SUET

year-round

SAW IT!

STAN'S COOL STUFF

Named for the yellow patch near its bill, this woodpecker likes to live in dry forests, in cottonwoods near water or in mesquite. Grasshoppers are one of its favorite foods! It saves food for later by hiding it behind tree bark (called caching).

Scissor-tailed Flycatcher

Look for the extremely long tail

FEMALE

What to look for:

white-to-gray head, neck, breast and back; black wings; bright pink underneath wings and on sides, which is easiest to see in flight; a very long black tail with patches of white

Where you'll find them:

open fields, prairies, scrubby areas, parks

Calls and songs:

a series of squeaks that sound a little like a squeaky toy

On the move:

male performs an up-down and zigzag courtship flight, showing off his long flowing tail; the flight sometimes ends with a reverse somersault

What they eat:

insects

Nest:

cup; Mom builds it

Eggs, chicks and childcare:

3–5 white eggs with brown and red markings; Mom incubates; Mom and Dad feed the young

Spends the winter:

Mexico and Central America

STAN'S COOL STUFF

This bird hunts for dragonflies and grasshoppers by waiting on a post or a low tree and then flying out to capture them as they pass by. It also hunts on the ground. It's easy to spot because of its super-long tail that looks like a pair of scissors!

Ring-necked Duck

Look for the white rings on the blue bill

MALE

FEMALE
pg. 119

What to look for:
handsome duck with a black head, chest and back, light gray-to-whitish sides, a blue bill with a thick white ring near the tip and a thinner white ring at the base; head is tall with a sloping forehead

Where you'll find them:
usually in larger freshwater lakes rather than saltwater marshes

Calls and songs:
male gives a quick series of grating barks and grunts; female gives high-pitched peeps

On the move:
dives underwater to forage for food; takes to flight by springing up off the water

What they eat:
aquatic plants and insects

Nest:
ground nest; Mom builds it

Eggs, chicks and childcare:
8–10 grayish-to-brown eggs; Mom incubates the eggs and teaches the young how to feed

Spends the winter:
in Texas and other southern states, the Caribbean, Mexico and Central America

REAL QUICK

Size
16–18"

Nest
GROUND

Feeder
NONE

winter

SAW IT!

STAN'S COOL STUFF

The Ring-necked Duck is a common winter duck throughout Texas. It's also called the Ring-billed Duck due to the obvious ring on its bill. Oddly enough, it was named for the faint rusty collar on its neck, which is nearly impossible to see.

American Avocet

Look for the long, thin upturned bill

BREEDING

WINTER

What to look for:
black and white back, white belly and long gray legs; a long, thin upturned bill; head and neck rusty red during breeding, and gray in the winter

Where you'll find them:
shallow wetlands, ponds, shallow lakes and coastlines and mudflats in the winter

Calls and songs:
a high pitched "keet, keet" repeated

On the move:
quickly walking in shallow water, often in small groups

What they eat:
insects, **crustaceans**, aquatic plants, fruit

Nest:
ground nest; Mom and Dad build it

Eggs, chicks and childcare:
3–5 light olive-colored eggs with brown markings; Mom and Dad sit on the eggs and feed the young

Spends the winter:
partial migrator to non-migrator in Texas

REAL QUICK

Size
18"

Nest
GROUND

Feeder
NONE

year-round
summer
migration

SAW IT!

STAN'S COOL STUFF

A shorebird with a long beak and even longer legs, the American Avocet uses its bill to search for insects and crustaceans in muddy water. Very protective of its nest, it will pretend to be hurt to draw a predator away, or it may scare one away by dive-bombing it!

Pileated Woodpecker

Look for the bright red crest

MALE

FEMALE

What to look for:
bright red crest that looks like a hat; bright red forehead and mustache, and a black back; female has a black forehead and lacks a red mustache

Where you'll find them:
prefers areas with lots of woodland

Calls and songs:
drums on hollow branches, chimneys and such to announce territory; loud, rapid "cuk-cuk-cuk" calls carry over a long distance

On the move:
white leading edge of wings flashes brightly during flight

What they eat:
insects (especially its favorite, carpenter ants); visits **suet** feeders and feeders with peanuts

Nest:
excavates cavity in a dead or live tree trunk

Eggs, chicks and childcare:
3–5 white eggs; Mom and Dad sit on the eggs and regurgitate bugs to feed the youngsters

Spends the winter:
doesn't **migrate**; stays in Texas year-round

REAL QUICK

Size
19"

Nest
CAVITY

Feeder
SUET

year-round

SAW IT!

STAN'S COOL STUFF

This is our largest woodpecker. It's shy, despite its size. It digs oval holes up to a few feet long in tree trunks, looking for bugs to eat. You'll see large wood chips at the base of those trees. The young come out of the nest looking and sounding just like the adults.

Osprey

Look for the dark line through the eyes

What to look for:
white chest, belly and head, with a dark eye line

Where you'll find them:
always near water, from rivers to wetlands

Calls and songs:
a high-pitched, whistle-like **call**, often given in flight as a warning

On the move:
can hover for a few seconds before diving to catch a fish; carries fish in a head-first position in flight for better aerodynamics

What they eat:
fish

Nest:
platform made with twigs; on a raised wooden platform, man-made tower or in a tall dead tree

Eggs, chicks and childcare:
2–4 white eggs with brown marks; parents sit on the eggs and feed the **hatchlings**

Spends the winter:
some **migrate** into Texas and other southern states, as well as Mexico and Central and South America

REAL QUICK

Size
21-24"

Nest
PLATFORM

Feeder
NONE

summer
migration
winter

SAW IT!

STAN'S COOL STUFF

The Osprey is the only species in its family. It is the only **raptor** that plunges feet-first into the water to catch fish. Bald Eagles (pg. 63) will harass it for its catch. At one time, it was almost extinct. It was reintroduced to many regions, and populations are now stable.

Crested Caracara

Look for the black crest

JUVENILE

SOARING

What to look for:
black body and wings with a white chin, upper neck and wing tips; large black crest; a large gray bill and an orange face; long yellow legs; white tail with a black band that is easiest to see in flight

Where you'll find them:
open scrubby areas, desert

Calls and songs:
mostly silent, can make a slow rattling sound

On the move:
glides with its wings held out flat; often seen with vultures, which hold their wings in a V shape

What they eat:
carrion, small mammals, insects, reptiles

Nest:
platform; Mom builds it

Eggs, chicks and childcare:
2–3 white or pinkish eggs with brown markings; Mom and Dad sit on the eggs and feed the young

Spends the winter:
in Texas; moves around to find food

REAL QUICK

Size
22-25"

Nest
PLATFORM

Feeder
NONE

year-round

SAW IT!

STAN'S COOL STUFF

This is the largest member of the falcon family. The Crested Caracara loves to eat roadkill, often flying low above roads at sunrise. It also hunts on the ground and chases after mice and other prey. It is often seen with vultures.

Bald Eagle

Look for the white head

JUVENILE

What to look for:

white head and tail, curved yellow bill and yellow feet; **juvenile** has white speckles and a gray bill

Where you'll find them:

often near water; likes open areas with daily food

Calls and songs:

weak, high-pitched screams, one after another

On the move:

a spectacular aerial mating **display** in which one eagle flips upside down and locks talons with another; both fall, tumbling down, then break apart and fly off

What they eat:

fish, **carrion** (dead rabbits and squirrels), birds (mainly ducks), prefers American Coots (pg. 29)

Nest:

massive platform of sticks, usually in a tree; nests used for many years can weigh up to 1,000 pounds

Eggs, chicks and childcare:

2–3 off-white eggs; Mom and Dad share all duties

Spends the winter:

some **migrate** into Texas and other southern states; others live in Texas year-round and do not leave

REAL QUICK

Size
31–37"

Nest
PLATFORM

Feeder
NONE

year-round
winter

SAW IT!

STAN'S COOL STUFF

Bald Eagles nearly became extinct, but they're doing well now. Their wingspan is huge, stretching out up to 7½ feet! They return to the same nest and add more sticks each year, enlarging it over time. The heads and tails of **juveniles** turn white at 4–5 years.

63

Mountain Bluebird

Look for the blue head, back, wings and tail

MALE

FEMALE

What to look for:
male is a sky blue bird with a darker blue head, back, wings and tail and a white lower belly; thin black bill; female is tan with blue on the wings and tail

Where you'll find them:
open mountainous country, prairies, fields

Calls and songs:
a simple warbling "churr," over and over

On the move:
perches while hunting; makes short direct flights

What they eat:
insects

Nest:
cavity; old woodpecker cavity, wooden nest box; Mom lines the cavity, making a cup for the eggs

Eggs, chicks and childcare:
4-6 pale blue eggs without markings; Mom sits on eggs; Mom and Dad feed the young

Spends the winter:
In Texas and other southwestern states; Mexico

Size
7"

Nest
CAVITY

Feeder
MEALWORM

winter

SAW ✓ IT!

STAN'S COOL STUFF

Not that long ago, bluebirds were in trouble because people cut down the dead trees bluebirds often use for their nests. Thankfully, bluebirds adapt well to nest boxes, and over the last 30 years, people have placed many of them, helping their populations recover.

Eastern Bluebird

Look for the rusty-red chest

MALE

FEMALE

What to look for:
male has a sky-blue head, back, wings and tail, with a rusty-red chest and white belly; female is grayer

Where you'll find them:
open habitats (prefers farm fields, pastures and roadsides), forest edges, parks and yards

Calls and songs:
male repeats a distinctive "chur-lee chur chur-lee" song mostly in spring as he displays to the female

On the move:
short flights from tree to tree; often perches in trees or on posts, dropping to ground to grab bugs

What they eat:
insects, fruit; visits mealworm and **suet** feeders

Nest:
cavity; adds a soft lining in an old woodpecker hole or a bluebird nest box

Eggs, chicks and childcare:
4–5 pale blue eggs; Mom incubates the eggs, and Dad and Mom feed the kids; 3 broods per year

Spends the winter:
in Texas and other southern states; moves just far enough south to avoid harsh winter weather

Size
7"

Nest
CAVITY

Feeder
MEALWORM

year-round
winter

SAW IT!

STAN'S COOL STUFF

The bluebird is a cousin of the American Robin (pg. 161). It was nearly eliminated due to a lack of tree cavities, but it's thriving now thanks to people who have put up bluebird nest boxes. The young of the first **brood** sometimes help care for the later broods.

Barn Swallow

Look for the deeply forked tail

What to look for:
  sleek blue-black back, rusty chin, cinnamon belly and a long, deeply forked tail

Where you'll find them:
  wetlands, farms, suburban yards and parks

Calls and songs:
  gives a twittering **warble** that's followed by a rapid mechanical sound

On the move:
  flaps continuously, often low over land or water; unlike other swallows, it rarely glides

What they eat:
  bugs—especially beetles, wasps (caught carefully) and flies

Nest:
  cup made of mud; brings in up to 1,000 beak-loads of mud to build nest, often on a building; usually it's in a **colony** of 4–6 birds; sometimes nests alone

Eggs, chicks and childcare:
  4–5 white eggs with brown marks; Mom sits on the eggs, and Mom and Dad feed the chicks

Spends the winter:
  in Central and South America

Size
7"

Nest
CUP

Feeder
NONE

summer

SAW IT!

STAN'S COOL STUFF

The Barn Swallow is the only swallow in Texas with a deeply forked tail. It drinks while flying low over water, and it sips the waterdrops on wet leaves. It bathes when it flies through rain or sprinklers. Usually it nests on a barn, house or under a bridge.

Blue Jay

Look for the large crest

What to look for:
vivid blue bird with a black **necklace**; a large crest, which the jay raises and lowers at will

Where you'll find them:
in the woods and all around your backyard

Calls and songs:
loud, noisy and mimics other birds; screams like a hawk around feeders to scare away other birds

On the move:
carries seeds and nuts in a pouch under its tongue during flight

What they eat:
insects, fruit, seeds, nuts, bird eggs and babies in other nests; visits seed feeders, ground feeders with corn and any feeder with peanuts

Nest:
cup of twigs in a tree, near the main trunk

Eggs, chicks and childcare:
4–5 speckled green-to-blue eggs; Mom sits on the eggs; Mom and Dad feed the little ones

Spends the winter:
in Texas; moves around to find an abundant source of food

REAL QUICK

Size
12"

Nest
CUP

Feeder
HOPPER

year-round
winter

SAW ✓ **IT!**

STAN'S COOL STUFF

Blue Jays are very intelligent. They store food in hiding places, called caches, to eat later. They can remember where they hide thousands of nuts! Jays are known as the alarm of the forest, screaming at intruders in the woods.

Tricolored Heron

Look for a blue-and-white neck

NON-BREEDING

What to look for:

blue-gray head, neck and wings, white on the neck and belly, yellow-to-green legs; a long blue bill with a dark tip during breeding season; non-breeding bill is gray

Where you'll find them:

wetland habitats; usually in saltwater marshes but also in freshwater marshes inland

Calls and songs:

gives a raspy nasal **call** if startled, then flies off

On the move:

hunts by standing still and waiting, but it will also chase after small fish

What they eat:

fish and aquatic insects

Nest:

platform; in a **colony** with other herons; one adult is always on duty at the nest

Eggs, chicks and childcare:

3–6 light blue eggs; Mom and Dad share the jobs of incubating and feeding the babies

Spends the winter:

many don't **migrate**; moves around to find food

REAL QUICK

Size
24-28"

Nest
PLATFORM

Feeder
NONE

year-round
summer
migration

SAW ✓ **IT!**

STAN'S COOL STUFF

The Tricolored Heron can be identified by its white undersides. Unlike other herons, it wasn't hunted for its plumes. But its numbers still declined due to the loss of wetland habitats. In Texas, it's less numerous in winter. It's known to wander as far as Kansas.

Look for the yellow on the wings

What to look for:
brown with a heavily streaked back, chest and belly, yellow wing bars and yellow at base of tail

Where you'll find them:
coniferous to **deciduous** forests, open fields

Calls and songs:
gives a series of high-pitched, wheezy calls; also gives a wheezing **twitter**

On the move:
moves around to visit feeders in flocks of up to 20 or more birds, often with other finch species; flashes yellow wing markings in flight

What they eat:
seeds, bugs; visits seed (especially thistle) feeders

Nest:
cup; builds nest in a conifer near the end of a branch, where needles are dense

Eggs, chicks and childcare:
3–4 speckled greenish-blue eggs; Mom incubates the eggs; Mom and Dad bring food to the kiddies

Spends the winter:
in Texas; common in some winters and rare in others, moving around to find food

REAL QUICK

Size
5"

Nest
CUP

Feeder
TUBE OR HOPPER

winter

SAW ✔ IT!

STAN'S COOL STUFF

The Pine Siskin is a finch that breeds in small groups. Nests in the group are often only a few feet apart. The male feeds the female during **incubation**. **Juveniles** have a yellow tint on their chests and chins, but they lose this by late summer of their first year.

House Finch

Look for the heavily streaked chest

FEMALE

MALE
pg. 193

What to look for:
brown bird with heavy streaks on a white chest

Where you'll find them:
forests, city and suburban areas, around homes, parks and farms

Calls and songs:
male sings a loud, cheerful warbling song

On the move:
moves around in small family units; never travels long distances

What they eat:
seeds, fruit and leaf buds; comes to seed feeders and feeders with a glop of grape jelly

Nest:
cup; but occasionally in a cavity; likes to nest in a hanging flower basket or on a front door wreath

Eggs, chicks and childcare:
4–5 pale blue eggs, lightly marked; Mom sits on the eggs and Dad feeds her while she incubates; Mom and Dad feed the **brood**

Spends the winter:
in Texas; moves around to find food

REAL QUICK

Size
5"

Nest
CUP

Feeder
TUBE OR HOPPER

year-round

SAW IT!

STAN'S COOL STUFF

The House Finch is very social and can be a common bird at feeders. It was introduced to New York from the western U.S. in the 1940s. Now it's found all across the country. Unfortunately, it suffers from a fatal eye disease that causes the eyes to crust over.

House Wren

Look for the slightly curved bill

What to look for:
brown bird with light brown marks on the wings and tail; a slightly curved brown bill

Where you'll find them:
brushy yards, woodlands, forest edges and parks

Calls and songs:
sings a lot; during the mating season, it sings from dawn to dusk

On the move:
short flights from protective bushes; holds its tail up briefly after landing

What they eat:
insects, spiders and snails

Nest:
cavity in a tree or birdhouse; easily attracted to a nest box; builds a twiggy nest in spring and lines it with pine needles and grass

Eggs, chicks and childcare:
4–6 tan eggs with brown marks; Mom and Dad incubate the eggs and raise the chicks

Spends the winter:
in Texas, other southern states and Mexico

REAL QUICK

Size
5"

Nest
CAVITY

Feeder
NONE

summer
migration
winter

SAW IT!

STAN'S COOL STUFF

The male chooses several nest cavities and puts a few small twigs in each. The female selects one cavity, and then fills it with short twigs. Often she will have trouble fitting long twigs through the entrance hole, but she'll try again and again until she's successful.

Carolina Wren

Look for the bold white eyebrows

What to look for:
 orange-yellow chest and belly, a white throat, bold white eyebrows, and a stubby tail, often held up

Where to find them:
 brushy yards and woodlands

Calls and songs:
 sings year-round; male sings up to 40 song types, singing one song repeatedly before switching to another; female also sings, resulting in duets

On the move:
 short, fast flights; often perching high up to sing before flying again

What they eat:
 insects, fruit and some seeds; comes to **suet** and mealworm feeders

Nest:
 cavity; nests in birdhouses and in unusual places, like mailboxes, car bumpers and broken taillights

Eggs, chicks and childcare:
 4–6 white (sometimes pink) eggs with brown marks; Mom incubates; parents feed the babies

Spends the winter:
 doesn't **migrate**; stays in Texas year-round

REAL QUICK

Size
5½"

Nest
CAVITY

Feeder
SUET OR MEALWORM

year-round

SAW IT!

STAN'S COOL STUFF

Carolina Wrens have a long-term **pair bond**. Mated pairs stay with each other in their territory all year long. They can have up to three broods per year. The male often takes over feeding the young when the female nests again.

Dark-eyed Junco

Look for the ivory-to-pink bill

FEMALE

MALE
pg. 149

What to look for:
plump bird with a tan-to-brown chest, head and back, a white belly and a tiny ivory-to-pink bill

Where you'll find them:
on the ground in small flocks with other juncos and sparrows

Calls and songs:
a beautiful, loud, musical **trill** lasting 2–3 seconds

On the move:
outermost tail feathers are white and appear as a white V during flight

What they eat:
seeds (scoffs down many weed seeds) and insects; visits ground and seed feeders

Nest:
cup on the ground in a wide variety of habitats; female chooses a well-hidden nest site

Eggs, chicks and childcare:
3–5 white eggs with reddish-brown marks; Mom incubates the eggs; Dad and Mom feed the babies

Spends the winter:
in Texas

REAL QUICK

Size
5½"

Nest
CUP

Feeder
GROUND

winter

SAW IT!

STAN'S COOL STUFF

The junco is one of our most common winter birds. Usually just the females are seen because they **migrate** farther south. This round, dark-eyed bird uses both feet at the same time to "**double-scratch**" the ground, exposing seeds and insects to eat.

House Sparrow

Look for the black throat patch

MALE

FEMALE

What to look for:
male has a brown back, gray belly and crown, large black patch from throat to chest; female is light brown with distinct light eyebrows and lacks a throat patch

Where you'll find them:
just about any **habitat**, from cities to farms

Calls and songs:
one of the first birds heard in cities during spring

On the move:
nearly always in small flocks

What they eat:
seeds, insects and fruit; comes to seed feeders

Nest:
cavity; uses dried grass, scraps of plastic, paper and whatever else is available to construct an oversized domed cup within the cavity

Eggs, chicks and childcare:
4–6 white eggs with brown marks; Mom sits on the eggs; Mom and Dad feed the little ones

Spends the winter:
doesn't **migrate**; stays in Texas year-round; moves around to find food

STAN'S COOL STUFF

The House Sparrow is very comfortable being around people. It was introduced to Central Park in New York City from Europe in 1850. It adjusted to nearly all habitats and now is seen across North America. Populations are decreasing in the U.S. and worldwide.

White-throated Sparrow

Look for the light stripes on the head

WHITE-STRIPED

TAN-STRIPED

What to look for:
striped head, white or tan throat patch and small yellow **lores** between the eyes

Where you'll find them:
bogs, evergreen and leafy forests, under feeders

Calls and songs:
sings a wonderful song all year and can even be heard at night, sounding like "oh-Canada, Canada"

On the move:
often hangs around on the ground with other sparrows during winter

What they eat:
insects, seeds and fruit; comes to ground feeders

Nest:
cup on the ground under a small tree

Eggs, chicks and childcare:
4–6 greenish, bluish or creamy-white eggs with reddish-brown marks; Mom incubates the eggs; Mom and Dad both take care of the babies

Spends the winter:
in Texas, other southern states and Mexico

REAL QUICK

Size
6-7"

Nest
CUP

Feeder
GROUND

migration
winter

SAW IT!

STAN'S COOL STUFF

This bird has two color variations: white-striped and tan-striped. Both variations mate with each other. Both variations also sing, except for the tan-striped females. This is odd, and scientists aren't sure why those females don't sing. Maybe you can figure it out.

Brown-headed Cowbird

Look for the pointed gray bill

FEMALE

MALE
pg. 19

What to look for:
  brown bird with a sharp, pointed gray bill

Where you'll find them:
  forest edges, open fields, farmlands and backyards

Calls and songs:
  sings a low, gurgling song that sounds like water moving; cowbird young are raised by other bird parents, but they still end up singing and calling like their own parents, without ever hearing them

On the move:
  Mom flies quietly to another bird's nest, swiftly lays an egg, then flies quickly away

What they eat:
  insects and seeds; visits seed feeders

Nest:
  doesn't nest; lays eggs in the nests of other birds

Eggs, chicks and childcare:
  white eggs with brown marks; the **host** bird incubates any number of cowbird eggs in her nest and feeds the cowbird young along with her own

Spends the winter:
  in Texas and other southern states

STAN'S COOL STUFF

Cowbirds are **brood parasites**, meaning they don't nest or raise their own families. Instead, they lay their eggs in other birds' nests, leaving the host birds to raise their young. Cowbirds have laid their eggs in the nests of more than 200 other bird species.

Cedar Waxwing

Look for the black mask

JUVENILE

What to look for:
sleek bird with a pointed crest, black mask, light yellow belly and waxy-looking red wing tips; tail has a bold yellow tip; **juvenile** lacks red wing tips

Where you'll find them:
treetops, forest edges, in trees with fruit

Calls and songs:
constantly makes a high-pitched "sreee" whistling sound while it's perched or in flight

On the move:
flies in flocks of 5–100 birds; moves from area to area, looking for berries

What they eat:
berry-like cedar cones, fruit, seeds and insects

Nest:
cup; Mom and Dad construct it together

Eggs, chicks and childcare:
4–6 pale blue eggs with brown marks; Mom sits on the eggs; Mom and Dad feed the little ones

Spends the winter:
in Texas; wanders around in search of available food supplies

REAL QUICK

Size
7½"

Nest
CUP

Feeder
NONE

winter

SAW IT!

STAN'S COOL STUFF

The waxwing is named for its waxy-looking red wing tips and for the cedar's small, blueberry-like cones that it likes to eat. Before berries are abundant, it eats bugs. The young obtain the mask after their first year of life and red wing tips after their second year.

Northern Cardinal

Look for the reddish bill

FEMALE

JUVENILE

MALE
pg. 197

What to look for:
tan-to-brown bird with a black mask and a large reddish bill; **juvenile** has a blackish-gray bill

Where you'll find them:
wide variety of habitats, including backyards and parks; usually likes thick **vegetation**

Calls and songs:
calls "whata-cheer-cheer-cheer" in spring; both female and male sing and give chip notes all year

On the move:
short flights from **cover**, often landing on the ground

What they eat:
loves sunflower seeds and enjoys insects, fruit, peanuts and **suet**; visits seed feeders

Nest:
cup of twigs and bark strips, often low in a tree

Eggs, chicks and childcare:
3–4 speckled bluish-white eggs; Mom and Dad share the incubating and feeding duties

Spends the winter:
doesn't **migrate**; gathers with other cardinals and moves around to find good sources of food

STAN'S COOL STUFF

The Northern Cardinal is one of the few species that has both female and male songsters. Like the males, females sing loud, complex songs. Cardinals are the first to arrive at feeders in the morning and the last to leave before dark.

Cactus Wren

Look for the white eyebrows

What to look for:
a speckled brown bird with bold white eyebrows, a brown crown and many dark spots on the upper chest to throat, often forming a central dark patch; a long tail and a large, slightly downward-curving bill

Where you'll find them:
desert areas

Calls and songs:
a loud "krr-krr-krr-krr-krr" or "cha-cha-cha-cha"

On the move:
male crouches, extends wings, fans tail and growls to female during courtship

What they eat:
insects, fruit, seeds; comes to seed or suet feeders and birdbaths

Nest:
covered cup; domed or ball-shaped; Mom and Dad build it

Eggs, chicks and childcare:
3–4 pale white-to-pink eggs with brown marks; Mom incubates; Mom and Dad feed the young

Spends the winter:
doesn't migrate; stays in Texas year-round

Nest
CUP

Feeder
SUET OR GROUND

year-round

SAW ✓ **IT!**

STAN'S COOL STUFF

The cactus wren got its name because it builds its nest in cholla or cactus. It lines its hollowed-out chamber with grasses and feathers. Pairs stay together all year, defending territory, but nesting inside a cactus certainly helps keep predators away too.

Eastern & Spotted Towhee

Look for the rusty sides

EASTERN FEMALE

MALE
pg. 23

SPOTTED FEMALE

MALE
pg. 23

What to look for:
   light brown bird with rusty sides, a white belly, red eyes, and a long brown tail with a white tip

Where to find them:
   shrubby areas with short trees and thick bushes, backyards and parks

Calls and songs:
   calls "tow-hee" distinctly; also has a characteristic **call** that sounds like "drink-your-tea"

On the move:
   short flights between shrubby areas and heavy **cover**; flashes white wing patches during flight

What they eat:
   insects, seeds and fruit; comes to ground feeders

Nest:
   cup; Mom constructs the nest

Eggs, chicks and childcare:
   3–4 creamy-white eggs with brown marks; Mom incubates the eggs; Dad and Mom feed the young

Spends the winter:
   in Texas and other southern states

Size
8½"

Nest
CUP

Feeder
GROUND

Eastern

Spotted

year-round
winter

SAW IT!

STAN'S COOL STUFF

The towhee is named for its distinctive "tow-hee" call. It hops backward with both feet, raking leaves to find insects and seeds. These two sparrow species are large, nearly the size of a robin. They often have up to three clutches of eggs each breeding season.

Red-winged Blackbird

Look for the white eyebrows

FEMALE

MALE
pg. 25

What to look for:
heavily streaked with a pointed brown bill and white (sometimes yellow) eyebrows

Where you'll find them:
around marshes, wetlands, lakes and rivers

Calls and songs:
male sings and repeats calls from cattail tops and the surrounding **vegetation**

On the move:
flocks with as many as 10,000 birds gather in autumn, often with other blackbirds

What they eat:
seeds in spring and autumn, insects in summer; visits seed and **suet** feeders

Nest:
cup; in a thick stand of cattails over shallow water

Eggs, chicks and childcare:
3–4 speckled bluish-green eggs; Mom does all the incubating, but both parents feed the babies

Spends the winter:
in Texas and other southern states, Mexico and Central America

SAW IT!

STAN'S COOL STUFF

During autumn and winter, thousands of these birds gather in farm fields, wetlands and marshes. Come spring, males sing to defend territories and show off their wing patches (**epaulets**) to the females. Later, males can be aggressive when defending their nests.

American Kestrel

Look for the black lines on the face

MALE

FEMALE

What to look for:
rusty back, blue-gray wings, spotted chest, two black lines on the face, a wide black band on the tip of tail; female has rusty wings, dark tail bands

Where you'll find them:
open fields, prairies, farm fields, along highways

Calls and songs:
loud series of high-pitched "klee-klee-klee" calls

On the move:
hovers in midair near roads, then dives for **prey**; pumps tail up and down after landing on a perch

What they eat:
bugs (especially grasshoppers), small animals and birds, reptiles

Nest:
cavity in a tree or wooden nest box; doesn't add nesting material

Eggs, chicks and childcare:
4–5 white eggs with brown marks; parents take turns sitting on the eggs and feeding the babies

Spends the winter:
in Texas and other southern states, Mexico and Central America

REAL QUICK

Size
9-11"

Nest
CAVITY

Feeder
NONE

year-round
winter

SAW **IT!**

STAN'S COOL STUFF

The kestrel is a small falcon that perches nearly upright. The male and female have different markings—this is unusual for a **raptor**. It can see **ultraviolet light**. That ability helps it find mice and other prey by their urine, which glows bright yellow in ultraviolet light.

Look for the two black neck bands

What to look for:
brown back, white belly, two black bands around the neck like a **necklace**; a bold reddish-orange rump, visible in flight

Where you'll find them:
open country, vacant fields, along railroad tracks, driveways, gravel pits and wetland edges

Calls and songs:
gives a very loud and distinctive "kill-deer" **call**

On the move:
fakes a broken wing to draw intruders away from the nest, and then takes flight once the nest is safe

What they eat:
loves bugs; also eats worms and snails

Nest:
ground nest; Dad makes just a slight depression in gravel, often very hard to see

Eggs, chicks and childcare:
3–5 tan eggs with brown marks; Dad and Mom incubate the eggs and lead the **hatchlings** to food

Spends the winter:
in Texas and other southern states, Mexico and Central America

REAL QUICK

Size
11"

Nest
GROUND

Feeder
NONE

year-round

SAW ✓ **IT!**

STAN'S COOL STUFF

Scientists group the Killdeer in the family of shorebirds, but you're more likely to spot one along railroad tracks, around farms and in other dry habitats than you are at the lakeshore. It's the only shorebird with two black neck bands. It migrates in small flocks.

103

Northern Flicker

Look for the black mustache

MALE

FEMALE

What to look for:
male is a brown-and-black bird with a black mustache and black **necklace**, a speckled chest and a red spot on the **nape** of neck; female lacks a black mustache

Where you'll find them:
forests, small woods, backyards, parks

Calls and songs:
gives a loud "wacka-wacka" **call**

On the move:
flies in a deep, exaggerated up-and-down pattern, flashing yellow under its wings and tail

What they eat:
insects (especially ants and beetles); known to eat the eggs of other birds; visits **suet** feeders

Nest:
cavity in a tree or in a nest box that is stuffed with sawdust; often reuses an old nest several times

Eggs, chicks and childcare:
5–8 white eggs; Mom and Dad incubate the eggs and feed the baby woodpeckers

Spends the winter:
in Texas and other southern states

REAL QUICK

Size
12"

Nest
CAVITY

Feeder
SUET

year-round
winter

SAW ✓ IT!

STAN'S COOL STUFF

The Northern Flicker is the only woodpecker to regularly feed on the ground. The male often picks the nest site, usually a natural cavity in a tree. Both parents will pitch in to dig as needed, taking as many as 12 days to finish excavating a hole.

Mourning Dove

Look for the small round head

What to look for:
brown-to-gray bird with shiny, **iridescent** pink and greenish-blue on the neck, a gray patch on the head, and black spots on the wings and tail

Where you'll find them:
around your seed and ground feeders, open fields

Calls and songs:
known for its soft, sad (mournful) cooing

On the move:
wind rushes through its wing feathers during takeoff and flight, creating a whistling sound

What they eat:
seeds; visits ground and seed feeders

Nest:
flimsy platform in a tree, made with twigs; often falls apart in a storm or during high winds

Eggs, chicks and childcare:
2 white eggs; parents incubate the eggs and feed a regurgitated liquid to their young for the first few days of life

Spends the winter:
in Texas and other southern states; will move around to find food

REAL QUICK

Size
12"

Nest
PLATFORM

Feeder
GROUND

year-round

SAW ✓ IT!

STAN'S COOL STUFF

The dove is a ground feeder that bobs its head as it walks. It's one of the few birds that drinks without lifting its head, like the Rock Pigeon (pg. 171). Parents **regurgitate** a liquid, called **crop-milk**, to feed to their young (**squab**) during their first few days of life.

Great-tailed Grackle

Look for the gray-to-brown belly

FEMALE

MALE
pg. 31

What to look for:
a brown bird with a gray-to-brown belly; light brown-to-white eyes, eyebrows, throat and upper portion of chest; **juvenile** similar to female

Where you'll find them:
open areas, backyards, parks

Calls and songs:
high-pitched, vibrating **call** given over and over

On the move:
seen around parking lots, in trees, and walking on the ground; often calling and chasing each other

What they eat:
insects, fruit, seeds; comes to seed feeders

Nest:
cup; Mom builds it

Eggs, chicks and childcare:
3–5 greenish blue eggs with brown markings; Mom incubates and feeds the young

Spends the winter:
stays in Texas all year; moves around to find food

STAN'S COOL STUFF

Great-tailed grackles nest in groups (called **colonies**); the nests are located in trees near lawns or pastures. Males don't help build the nests, incubate eggs or raise young. Females often use materials created by humans, such as plastic or paper, in their nests!

109

Look for the boldly patterned wings

BREEDING

WINTER
pg. 173

What to look for:
brown bird with a white belly, and brown legs and bill; distinctive black-and-white pattern on the wings, seen flashing in flight or during **display**

Where you'll find them:
at the beach

Calls and songs:
calls "pill-will-willet" during the breeding season; gives a "kip-kip-kip" alarm **call** as it takes flight

On the move:
easy to identify due to the black-and-white wing pattern that flashes when the bird flaps rapidly

What they eat:
insects, small fish, small crabs, worms and clams

Nest:
ground nest; Mom builds the nest

Eggs, chicks and childcare:
3–5 olive-colored eggs with dark marks; parents sit on the eggs and feed the young

Spends the winter:
in coastal Texas, other Gulf Coast states and coastal South America

REAL QUICK

Size
14–16"

Nest
GROUND

Feeder
NONE

**year-round
migration**

SAW IT!

STAN'S COOL STUFF

This bird is seen along the coast and is very common on beaches all winter. It is a medium-sized sandpiper that uses its long bill to probe into sand in search of food. It nests on the ground along the East and Gulf coasts, in some western states and in Canada.

Blue-winged Teal

Look for the white crescent on the face

MALE

FEMALE

What to look for:
brown duck with black speckles, a gray head with a white crescent on the face, a white patch on tail and blue wing patch (**speculum**); female is duller; lacks a white facial crescent and white patch on the tail

Where you'll find them:
wetlands and lakes

Calls and songs:
male makes a high-pitched squeak; female quacks

On the move:
direct flight to and from water; flocks fly fast in tight formation; female performs a **display** to draw predators away from the nest and young

What they eat:
aquatic plants, seeds and aquatic bugs

Nest:
cozy ground nest some distance from the water

Eggs, chicks and childcare:
8–11 creamy-white eggs; Mom does the **incubation** and feeds the ducklings

Spends the winter:
in Texas and other southern states, Mexico and Central America; non-migrator in parts of Texas

STAN'S COOL STUFF

This is one of the smallest ducks in North America. It migrates farther than most other ducks, nesting as far north as Alaska. The name "Blue-winged" refers to its blue wing patch, which is easiest to see when the bird is in flight.

Red-shouldered Hawk

Look for the reddish shoulders

What to look for:
cinnamon-red head, shoulders, chest and belly, brown wings and back with white spots, and a long tail with black-and-white bands; reddish wing linings, which are seen in flight

Where you'll find them:
wooded backyards, forest edges, woodlands

Calls and songs:
extremely vocal; gives distinctive loud screams

On the move:
alternates flapping with gliding

What they eat:
reptiles, amphibians, large insects and small birds

Nest:
large platform made of sticks and lined with sprigs of evergreen or other soft materials; usually in a fork of a large tree

Eggs, chicks and childcare:
2–4 white eggs with dark marks; Mom and Dad sit on the eggs and provide for the youngsters

Spends the winter:
in Texas; moves around in winter

REAL QUICK

Size
15-19"

Nest
PLATFORM

Feeder
NONE

year-round
winter

SAW ✓ **IT!**

STAN'S COOL STUFF

A common hawk in Texas, it likes to hunt along forest edges and will search for snakes, frogs, bugs and other **prey** as it perches. It stays in the same territory for many years. The parents start to build a nest in February. The young leave the nest (**fledge**) by June.

115

Barn Owl

Look for the heart-shaped face

What to look for:
a round head (without any "ears"); a rusty brown back of head, back, wings and tail; a heart-shaped white face, outlined in darker rusty brown; white chest and belly and dark eyes; long gray legs and gray feet; yellow bill; female similar to male, but often a bit more rusty looking on the chest and belly

Where you'll find them:
ranches, farms, suburbs and cities

Calls and songs:
doesn't hoot; instead, gives a long harsh scream (mostly it's the males that do this)

On the move:
associated with barns and abandoned buildings

What they eat:
small mammals, birds, snakes

Nest:
cavity; occasionally on a cliff crevice

Eggs, chicks and childcare:
3–7 white eggs without marks; Mom sits on eggs; Mom and Dad feed the young

Spends the winter:
in Texas

REAL QUICK

Size
16"

Nest
CAVITY

Feeder
NONE

year-round

SAW ✓ IT!

STAN'S COOL STUFF

This owl gets its name because it often nests in old barns, but it will nest in any dark cavity on cliffs. Active at night, barn owls can be common in cities and towns, but they may go unseen. Barn owls are important predators of mice, rats and other mammals.

117

King-necked Duck

Look for the white ring on the bill

FEMALE

MALE
pg. 53

What to look for:
overall brown with a brown back, light brown sides and dark brown crown; face is gray with a white eye-ring; bill has a white ring near the tip, and head is tall with a sloping forehead

Where you'll find them:
usually in larger freshwater lakes rather than saltwater marshes

Calls and songs:
female gives high-pitched peeps; male gives a quick series of grating barks and grunts

On the move:
dives underwater to forage for food; takes to flight by springing up off the water

What they eat:
aquatic plants and insects

Nest:
ground nest; Mom builds it

Eggs, chicks and childcare:
8–10 grayish-to-brown eggs; Mom incubates the eggs and teaches the young how to feed

Spends the winter:
in Texas and other southern states, the Caribbean, Mexico and Central America

REAL QUICK

Size
16–18"

Nest
GROUND

Feeder
NONE

winter

SAW ✓ IT!

STAN'S COOL STUFF

The Ring-necked Duck is one of the most abundant winter ducks in Texas. It's also called the Ring-billed Duck due to the obvious ring on its bill. Oddly enough, it was named for the faint rusty collar on its neck, which is nearly impossible to see.

Redhead

Look for the black tip on the bill

FEMALE

MALE
pg. 199

What to look for:
female is a plain brown duck with gray-to-white wing linings; round head; two-toned bill that is gray with a black tip

Where you'll find them:
wetlands, ponds, lakes, and rivers

Calls and songs:
a wheezy cat-like meow

On the move:
small flocks in fast flight

What they eat:
seeds, aquatic plants, insects

Nest:
ground nest; Mom usually builds it directly on the water's surface using large mats of **vegetation**

Eggs, chicks and childcare:
9–14 pale white eggs without marks; Mom incubates; Mom shows the young what to eat

Spends the winter:
in Texas, near water

REAL QUICK

Size
18–20"

Nest
GROUND

Feeder
NONE

winter

SAW ✔ **IT!**

STAN'S COOL STUFF

This duck dives into the water to find its food, mostly plants, seeds, and insects and other critters that live in the water. Female Redhead ducks are also a bit sneaky; they lay up to 75 percent of their eggs in the nests of other Redheads and other ducks!

Mallard

Look for the orange-and-black bill

FEMALE

MOTTLED DUCK

MALE pg. 187

What to look for:
overall brown duck with an orange-and-black bill, a white tail, and a blue-and-white wing mark (**speculum**), seen best in flight

Where you'll find them:
lakes and ponds, rivers and streams, and maybe even your backyard

Calls and songs:
the sound a duck makes is based on the female Mallard's classic quack; the male doesn't quack

On the move:
sometimes in huge flocks with hundreds of ducks; mostly in small flocks of 6–10, especially in spring

What they eat:
seeds, aquatic plants and insects; visits ground feeders offering corn

Nest:
ground nest; Mom builds it from plants nearby

Eggs, chicks and childcare:
7–10 greenish-to-whitish eggs; Mom incubates the eggs and leads the young to food

Spends the winter:
in Texas and other southern states

REAL QUICK

Size
19–21"

Nest
GROUND

Feeder
GROUND

year-round
winter

SAW ✓ **IT!**

STAN'S COOL STUFF

This is a dabbling duck, tipping forward in shallow water to feed on aquatic plants on the bottom. It will return to its birthplace each year. The Mottled Duck (see inset) looks very much like the female Mallard except for the bill color.

123

Northern Shoveler

Look for the large, shovel-like bill

FEMALE

MALE
pg. 189

What to look for:

brown duck with black speckles, green wing mark (**speculum**) and a super-large, spoon-shaped bill

Size
19-21"

Nest
GROUND

Feeder
NONE

winter

Where you'll find them:

shallow wetlands, ponds and small lakes

Calls and songs:

female gives a classic quack; male gives a crazy-sounding combination of popping and quacking, calling, "puk-puk, puk-puk, puk-puk"

On the move:

swims in tight circles, stirring up insects to eat; small flocks of 5–10 birds swim with bills pointing toward the water; flocks fly in tight formation

What they eat:

enjoys aquatic insects; likes plants, too

Nest:

ground nest; Mom forms plant material into a circle

Eggs, chicks and childcare:

9–12 olive-colored eggs; Mom sits on the eggs and leads her little shovelers to food

Spends the winter:

in Texas and other southern states, the Caribbean, Mexico and Central America

SAW ✓ **IT!**

STAN'S COOL STUFF

The Northern Shoveler is a medium-sized duck. It is the only shoveler species found in North America. The name "Shoveler" refers to its peculiar, shovel-like bill. It feeds by using its bill to sift tiny aquatic insects and plants floating on the water's surface.

Harris's Hawk

Look for the rusty brown shoulders

SOARING

JUVENILE

What to look for:
a dark brown hawk with rusty brown shoulders; black tail with a bright white tip; a bright white rump; yellow base of bill; long yellow legs and feet; rusty wing linings, best seen in flight; female same as male, but slightly larger

Where you'll find them:
woodlands near water; common in city parks and suburban yards

Calls and songs:
a raspy, grating **call**

On the move:
seen perching high up looking for prey; often seen in small groups

What they eat:
small mammals, snakes, birds, large insects

Nest:
platform; Mom and Dad build it

Eggs, chicks and childcare:
3–4 pale white eggs with some brown marks; Mom and Dad sit on the eggs and feed the young

Spends the winter:
in Texas

REAL QUICK

Size
19–21"

Nest
PLATFORM

Feeder
NONE

year-round

SAW IT!

STAN'S COOL STUFF

Unlike most raptors, it hunts in small groups, usually with other members of its family. Hunting as a team is easier than hunting alone. It helps them capture larger animals, such as jackrabbits. This is one of the more common hawks at wildlife education centers.

Red-tailed Hawk

Look for the rusty-red tail

What to look for:
plumage varies, but it's often brown with a white chest, brown belly band and a rusty-red tail

Where you'll find them:
just about anywhere; open country, where it flies over open fields and roadsides; cities, where it perches on freeway light posts, fences and trees

Calls and songs:
gives a high-pitched scream that trails off

On the move:
hunts in flight, flying in circles as it searches for **prey**

What they eat:
mice and other mammals, birds, snakes, large bugs

Nest:
large platform made of sticks, lined with materials such as evergreen needles; often in a large tree

Eggs, chicks and childcare:
2–3 white eggs, sometimes speckled; parents sit on the eggs and provide for the youngsters

Spends the winter:
in Texas

REAL QUICK

Size
19-23"

Nest
PLATFORM

Feeder
NONE

year-round

SAW IT!

STAN'S COOL STUFF

This **raptor** is a large hawk with a wide variety of colors from bird to bird, ranging from chocolate to nearly all white. The red color of the tail develops in the second year of life and usually is best seen from above. It returns to the same nest site each year.

Barred Owl

Look for the dark eyes

What to look for:
brown-to-gray owl with dark brown eyes, dark horizontal bars on upper chest, vertical streaks on the lower chest and belly, yellow bill and feet

Where you'll find them:
dense woodlands

Calls and songs:
gives calls of 6–8 hoots, sounding something like "who-who-who-cooks-for-you"

On the move:
a smooth and silent flight, gliding on flat, out-stretched wings; often hunts during the day, perching and watching for mice and other **prey**

What they eat:
small mammals, birds, fish, reptiles, amphibians

Nest:
natural cavity in a tree or uses a nest box with a large entrance hole; doesn't add nesting material

Eggs, chicks and childcare:
2–3 white eggs; Mom sits on the eggs; Mom and Dad attend to the babies

Spends the winter:
doesn't **migrate**; stays in Texas year-round

REAL QUICK

Size
20–24"

Nest
CAVITY

Feeder
NONE

year-round

SAW ✓ **IT!**

STAN'S COOL STUFF

It's a chunky bird with a large head. It fishes by hovering over water, and then reaches down to grab a fish. After the young **fledge**, they stay with their parents for up to four months.

Great Horned Owl

Look for the feather tufts on the head

What to look for:
"eared" owl with large yellow eyes, a V-shaped white marking and horizontal bars on the chest

Where you'll find them:
just about any **habitat** throughout Texas

Calls and songs:
calls a familiar "hoo-hoo-hoo-hoooo"

On the move:
flies silently on big wings that stretch out to 4 feet across; takes a few quick flaps, and then glides

What they eat:
small to medium mammals, birds (especially ducks), snakes and insects

Nest:
no nest; takes over the nest of another bird or uses a broken tree stump or other semi-cavity

Eggs, chicks and childcare:
2–3 white eggs, laid in early December, January or February; Mom incubates; Dad and Mom feed the **hatchlings**

Spends the winter:
doesn't **migrate** and usually hangs around the same area year after year

SAW ✓ **IT!**

STAN'S COOL STUFF

The "**horns**" of the Great Horned are feather tufts, not ears. Its eyelids close from the top down, like ours. It has fabulous hearing and can hear a mouse moving under a deep pile of leaves. It's one of the few animals that will kill a skunk or a porcupine.

Greater Roadrunner

Look for the crest

What to look for:
brown with white streaks; has a crest that can be raised and lowered; an extremely long tail and a long, pointed brown bill; blue patch just behind eyes; long gray legs with large feet

Where you'll find them:
just about any habitat

Calls and songs:
slow, descending low-pitched "coo-coo-coo-coo"

On the move:
quick burst of running, then stands still

What they eat:
insects, reptiles, small mammals and birds

Nest:
platform; low in a tree, shrub or cactus; Mom and Dad build it

Eggs, chicks and childcare:
4–6 white eggs without marks; Mom and Dad incubate the eggs and feed the young

Spends the winter:
in Texas

REAL QUICK

Size
23"

Nest
PLATFORM

Feeder
NONE

year-round

SAW IT!

STAN'S COOL STUFF

This bird is famous for living on the ground and running quickly, up to 18 miles per hour (29 km). One tough bird, it sometimes even eats rattlesnakes! It flies for short distances, usually in a low glide after a running takeoff.

Wild Turkey

Look for the bare blue-and-red head

MALE

FEMALE

What to look for:
funny-looking brown-and-bronze bird; bare blue-and-red head, long thin beard, and large fanning tail; female is thinner, duller and often lacks a beard

Where you'll find them:
just about any **habitat**, from suburban yards to prairies and forests

Calls and songs:
a fast, descending "gobble-gobble-gobble-gobble" that's often heard before the bird is seen

On the move:
a strong flier that can approach 60 mph; also able to fly straight up, and then away

What they eat:
insects, seeds and fruit

Nest:
ground nest; Mom scrapes out a shallow depression and pads it with soft leaves

Eggs, chicks and childcare:
10–12 whitish eggs with dull brown marks; Mom sits on the eggs and leads the babies to food

Spends the winter:
moves around Texas to find **cover** and food

REAL QUICK

Size
36–48"

Nest
GROUND

Feeder
NONE

year-round

SAW ✓ **IT!**

STAN'S COOL STUFF

The turkey is the largest native game bird in Texas. It sees three times better than people, and it can hear sounds from a mile away. A male will lead a group of up to 20 females. The male's head and neck change color when displaying for females.

137

Brown Pelican

Look for the huge gray bill

NON-BREEDING

What to look for:
gray-brown body with a black belly, a very long gray bill, a white or yellow head, and dark rusty-red on the back of the neck during breeding season; non-breeding back of the neck is white

Where you'll find them:
at the beach

Calls and songs:
no calls; snaps the upper bill and lower bill together to make a loud popping sound

On the move:
often sits on posts at beachside docks

What they eat:
fish; occasionally amphibians and eggs

Nest:
ground nest; in a large **colony**, often on an island

Eggs, chicks and childcare:
2–4 white eggs; Mom and Dad incubate the eggs and share the childcare

Spends the winter:
along coastal Texas

STAN'S COOL STUFF

A coastal bird of Texas, it was endangered not long ago due to the use of pesticides. It hunts by diving headfirst into the ocean. Then it opens its bill and sweeps fish into its mouth with the expandable pouch on the bottom of its bill, like a net.

Verdin

Look for the bright yellow head

MALE

FEMALE

JUVENILE

What to look for:
light gray to silvery overall; yellow head; short, pointed dark bill; dark legs and feet

Where you'll find them:
in thorny scrub plants and deserts

Calls and songs:
a quick and simple whistle call

On the move:
actively flitting around shrubs, small trees

What they eat:
seeds, insects, fruit, **nectar**

Nest:
covered cup; Dad builds it; the sturdy nests can last for a long time

Eggs, chicks and childcare:
4–5 bluish-green eggs with brown markings; Mom sits on the eggs; Mom and Dad feed the young

Spends the winter:
doesn't migrate; in Texas

REAL QUICK

Size
4¹/₂"

Nest
CUP

Feeder
NECTAR

year-round

SAW IT!

STAN'S COOL STUFF

A very friendly bird, it can be a regular visitor to nectar feeders and orange halves. The male builds several ball-shaped nests of thorny twigs, weaving in leaves and grass. The verdin is tiny, weighing just under seven grams—that's less than three pennies!

Carolina Chickadee

Look for the black cap

What to look for:
mostly gray bird with a black cap and throat patch, tan sides and belly, and a whitish chest

Where you'll find them:
nearly all habitats—just look around for this bird

Calls and songs:
calls "chika-dee-dee-dee-dee"; also gives a high-pitched, two-toned "fee-bee" **call** during spring; can have different calls in different regions

On the move:
flies short distances with short, fluttery wings

What they eat:
seeds, bugs and fruit; visits seed and **suet** feeders

Nest:
excavates a natural cavity or uses a nest box; gathers moss for the nest and fur to line it

Eggs, chicks and childcare:
5–7 white eggs with reddish-brown marks; Mom and Dad sit on the eggs and feed their **brood**

Spends the winter:
doesn't **migrate**; moves around to find food and shelter instead

REAL QUICK

Size
5"

Nest
CAVITY

Feeder
TUBE OR SUET

year-round

SAW ✓ IT!

STAN'S COOL STUFF

You can attract this bird with a seed feeder or a nest box. Usually it's the first to find a new feeder. It's easily tamed and hand-fed. Much of its diet comes from bird feeders, so it can be a common urban bird. It's often seen with nuthatches, woodpeckers and other birds.

143

White-breasted Nuthatch

Look for the white chest

MALE

FEMALE

What to look for:
male has a gray back with a white face, chest and belly, a black cap and **nape** of neck, and a large white patch on the rump; female is similar except with a gray cap and nape

Where you'll find them:
woodlands, parks, backyards, forest edges

Calls and songs:
a characteristic spring **call**, "whi-whi-whi-whi," given during February and March

On the move:
climbs down tree trunks headfirst, looking for hidden insects; quick, short flights from tree to tree

What they eat:
insects, insect eggs, seeds; visits seed and **suet** feeders

Nest:
cavity; Mom and Dad build a nest in an empty woodpecker hole or a natural cavity

Eggs, chicks and childcare:
5–7 white eggs with brown marks; Mom sits on the eggs; Mom and Dad feed the little ones

Spends the winter:
in Texas; moves around to find food

REAL QUICK

Size
5-6"

Nest
CAVITY

Feeder
TUBE OR SUET

year-round

SAW ✓ IT!

STAN'S COOL STUFF

The White-breasted Nuthatch has an extra-long hind toe claw, called a nail, on each foot, giving it the ability to cling to trees and climb down headfirst. It's often seen in flocks with chickadees. Pairs stay together all year and defend their territory.

Yellow-rumped Warbler

Look for the bright yellow patches

MALE

FEMALE

FIRST WINTER

What to look for:

gray with black streaks on the chest and yellow patches on head, flanks and rump; female is duller gray; first-winter **juvenile** is similar to the female

Where you'll find them:

can be seen in any **habitat** during migration; seems to prefer **deciduous** forests and forest edges

Calls and songs:

sings a wonderful song in spring; calls a single robust "chip," heard mostly during migration

On the move:

quickly moves among trees and from the ground to trees; flits around upper branches of tall trees

What they eat:

insects and berries; visits **suet** feeders in spring

Nest:

cup; Mom builds the nest on her own in forests

Eggs, chicks and childcare:

4–5 white eggs with brown marks; Mom sits on the eggs; Mom and Dad feed the young

Spends the winter:

in Texas, other southern states and Mexico and Central America

SAW IT!

STAN'S COOL STUFF

This bird is also called the Myrtle Warbler. It is one of the last warblers to arrive in winter and one of the first to leave in spring. The male molts his gray feathers in fall, changing to a dull color like the female for the winter. He keeps his yellow patches all year.

Dark-eyed Junco

Look for the pink bill

MALE

FEMALE
pg. 83

What to look for:
plump bird with a gray-to-charcoal chest, head and back, a white belly and a tiny pink bill

Where you'll find them:
on the ground in small flocks with other juncos and sparrows

Calls and songs:
a beautiful, loud, musical **trill** lasting 2–3 seconds

On the move:
outermost tail feathers are white and appear as a white V during flight

What they eat:
seeds (scoffs down many weed seeds) and insects; visits ground and seed feeders

Nest:
cup on the ground in a wide variety of habitats; female chooses a well-hidden nest site

Eggs, chicks and childcare:
3–5 white eggs with reddish-brown marks; Mom incubates the eggs; Dad and Mom feed the babies

Spends the winter:
in Texas; the arrival of the junco signals the start of winter

REAL QUICK

Size
5½"

Nest
CUP

Feeder
GROUND

winter

SAW IT!

STAN'S COOL STUFF

The junco is one of our most common winter birds. Usually just the females are seen here because they **migrate** farther south. This round, dark-eyed bird uses both feet at the same time to **"double-scratch"** the ground, exposing seeds and insects to eat.

149

Black-crested & Tufted Titmouse

Look for the black or gray pointed crest

TUFTED

BLACK-CRESTED

What to look for:
gray bird with a white chest and belly; the Black-crested Titmouse has a pointed black crest; the Tufted Titmouse has a gray crest

Where to find them:
woodlands, backyards and parks

Calls and songs:
quickly repeats a loud "peter-peter-peter" **call**

On the move:
usually seen only one or two at a time, never in big flocks, moving through thick forests and along forest edges

What they eat:
insects, seeds (especially black oil sunflower seeds) and fruit; visits seed and **suet** feeders

Nest:
cavity

Eggs, chicks and childcare:
5–7 white eggs with brown marks; Mom sits on the eggs, and Mom and Dad feed the young

Spends the winter:
doesn't **migrate**; stays in Texas year-round

REAL QUICK

Size
6"

Nest
CAVITY

Feeder
TUBE OR SUET

Tufted

Black-crested

year-round

SAW ✓ **IT!**

STAN'S COOL STUFF

A common feeder bird, its name means "small bird." Even though it is small, this bird is brave. It pulls hair from sleeping dogs, cats or squirrels and uses it to line the inside of its nest in an old woodpecker hole or a nest box.

Vermilion Flycatcher

Look for the pink belly to under the tail

FEMALE

MALE
pg. 195

What to look for:
a mostly gray bird with a gray head, neck and back; nearly white chin and chest; pink on belly and underneath tail; black tail; a thin black bill

Where you'll find them:
parks and open areas with trees, wetlands, scrub

Calls and songs:
a rapid series of high-pitched calls

On the move:
often seen perched low on a tree, pumping its tail up and down while waiting for a flying insect; it flies out to snatch it, then perches again to eat

What they eat:
insects

Nest:
cup; Mom builds it

Eggs, chicks and childcare:
2–4 white eggs with brown marks; Mom and Dad incubate the eggs and feed the young

Spends the winter:
a few stay in the most southern part of Texas; in Mexico

REAL QUICK

Size
6"

Nest
CUP

Feeder
NONE

summer
winter

SAW IT!

STAN'S COOL STUFF

Vermilion (*ver-mill-yun*) is another word for bright red, but only the male flycatcher is brightly colored. The female is mostly a drab gray. As you might have guessed, these birds eat a lot of bugs, especially bees, beetles, flies and grasshoppers.

Eastern Screech-Owl

Look for the feathered "ear" tufts

GRAY MORPH

RED MORPH

What to look for:
small "eared" owl with two different color variations: gray-and-white and red-and-white

Where you'll find them:
any type of forest, as long as it has some natural cavities suitable for roosting and nesting

Calls and songs:
a trembling, descending **trill**, like a sound effect in a scary movie; seldom gives a screeching **call**

On the move:
flies silently on short, rapidly flapping wings; active from dusk to dawn

What they eat:
large insects, small mammals, birds and snakes

Nest:
cavity; uses an old woodpecker hole or a wooden nest box and doesn't add nesting material

Eggs, chicks and childcare:
4–5 white eggs; Mom sits on the eggs to incubate; Dad feeds Mom and the newly hatched babies

Spends the winter:
doesn't **migrate**; stays in Texas year-round but has a different territory in winter than in summer

Size
8–10"

Nest
CAVITY

Feeder
NONE

year-round

SAW IT!

STAN'S COOL STUFF

This little owl has excellent hearing and eyesight. On winter days, it will sun itself at a nest entrance hole. The male and female may roost with each other at night and may have a long-term **pair bond**. The gray **morph** is more common than the red variety.

Loggerhead Shrike

Look for the black mask

What to look for:
gray head and back with a white chin, chest and belly; black wings, tail, legs and feet, with a black mask across the eyes; a hooked black bill

Where you'll find them:
coniferous trees, barbed wire fences and bird feeders, where it hunts small birds

Calls and songs:
doesn't sing; repeats harsh phrases lacking melody

On the move:
to hunt, it swoops down on **prey**, grasps it with the feet, hammers at it with its bill and carries it to a storage spot, where it's kept for eating later

What they eat:
insects (especially grasshoppers), lizards, small mammals and birds, frogs

Nest:
cup; Dad and Mom build it together

Eggs, chicks and childcare:
4–7 off-white eggs with dark marks; Mom sits on the eggs; Mom and Dad feed the baby birds

Spends the winter:
migrants join the many year-round residents

REAL QUICK

Size
9"

Nest
CUP

Feeder
NONE

year-round

SAW IT!

STAN'S COOL STUFF

The shrike is a songbird that's also called the Butcher Bird. It acts more like a **raptor** than a songster. It has weak feet, so it skewers its prey on thorns or other sharp objects. This helps it store the item for later and keeps it still when it tears off pieces to eat.

157

Pyrrhuloxia

Look for the red-tipped crest

MALE

FEMALE

What to look for:
male is gray overall with a bright red-tipped crest, a red mask, throat, breast, belly and red edges to the wings and tail; female is similar to male, less red; large yellow bill; dark eyes

Where you'll find them:
dry areas with brush; parks, backyards

Calls and songs:
has a loud, crisp song similar to a cardinal's and makes a single metallic "chip" **call**

On the move:
short and quick flights to thick cover

What they eat:
seeds, fruit, insects; will visit birdbaths and ground feeders

Nest:
cup; Mom builds it

Eggs, chicks and childcare:
2–4 gray-to-green eggs with brown marks; Mom and Dad incubate the eggs and feed the young

Spends the winter:
in Texas

Size
9"

Nest
CUP

Feeder
GROUND

year-round

SAW IT!

STAN'S COOL STUFF

Like its cousin, the Northern Cardinal, this bird (whose name is pronounced *peer-uh-lox-ia-uh*) is most active in early morning and just before sunset. Small flocks move around in the winter to find food, so you may see more than one at a time.

American Robin

Look for the rusty-red breast

MALE

FEMALE

What to look for:
black head and a rich, rusty-red breast; female is duller with a gray head and lighter breast

Where you'll find them:
loves to hop on lawns in search of worms

Calls and songs:
chips and chirps; sings all night in spring; studies report that city robins sing louder than country robins so they can be heard over traffic and noise

On the move:
found all over the U.S. in an amazing range of habitats, from sea level to mountaintops

What they eat:
insects, fruit and berries, as well as earthworms

Nest:
cup; weaves plant materials and uses mud to plaster the nest to a sheltered location

Eggs, chicks and childcare:
4–7 pale blue eggs; Mom sits on the eggs; Mom and Dad feed the baby robins

Spends the winter:
in Texas, other southern states and Mexico and Central America

REAL QUICK

Size
9–11"

Nest
CUP

Feeder
NONE

year-round
winter

SAW IT!

STAN'S COOL STUFF

When a robin walks across your lawn and turns its head to the side, it isn't listening for worms—it is looking for them. Because its eyes are on the sides of its head, a robin must focus its sight out of one eye to see the moving dirt caused by a worm.

Northern Mockingbird

Look for the white wing patches

What to look for:

silver-gray head and back, a light gray chest and belly, white wing patches, a mostly black tail with white outer tail feathers

Where to find them:

on top of a shrub, where it sits for long periods; parks and yards

Calls and songs:

imitates or mocks other birds (vocal mimicry); young males often sing at night

On the move:

very lively, spreading its wings, flashing its white wing patches and wagging its tail; wing patches flash during flight or **display**

What they eat:

insects and fruit

Nest:

cup; Mom and Dad work together to build it

Eggs, chicks and childcare:

3–5 speckled blue-green eggs; Mom sits on the eggs to incubate; Mom and Dad feed their young

Spends the winter:

in Texas and other southern states

REAL QUICK

Size
10"

Nest
CUP

Feeder
NONE

year-round

SAW IT!

STAN'S COOL STUFF

Mockingbirds perform a fantastic mating dance. Pairs hold up their heads and tails and run toward each other. They flash their wing patches, and then retreat to nearby **cover**. Usually they're not afraid of people, so you may be able to get a close look.

163

Curve-billed Thrasher

Look for the long downward-curved bill

What to look for:
large-bodied bird with a long tail; a long bill that curves downward; gray to light brown with faint spots on chest and belly

Where you'll find them:
familiar backyard bird that prefers scrubby desert habitat with mesquite, cactus or cholla

Calls and songs:
calls a loud "whit-wee"; male follows female during courtship, singing a soft song

On the move:
takes off with a short sprint followed by a hop

What they eat:
insects, fruit, seeds; comes to seed feeders on the ground and birdbaths

Nest:
cup; Mom and Dad build it

Eggs, chicks and childcare:
3–4 pale blue-green eggs with brown marks; Mom and Dad incubate and feed the young

Spends the winter:
in Texas

STAN'S COOL STUFF

This bird feeds on the ground and builds its nest in a spiny shrub or cactus, using twigs and grass. It will often reuse the nest after making minor repairs, and pairs often remain together all year. It will chase away any Cactus Wrens in the area.

White-winged Dove

Look for the white edges on the wings

What to look for:
light gray to brown with a white edge on the wings that's easy to see; small black dash underneath the cheeks; bright blue eye-rings around bright red eyes

Where you'll find them:
just about any open habitat

Calls and songs:
gives a distinctive call, "coo-cuk-ca-roo"

On the move:
fast wing flaps but slower flight

What they eat:
seeds, fruit; will come to seed feeders

Nest:
platform; Mom and Dad build it

Eggs, chicks and childcare:
2–4 white eggs without marks; Mom and Dad incubate the eggs and feed the young

Spends the winter:
partial migrator to non-migrator in Texas

Size
11"

Nest
PLATFORM

Feeder
GROUND

year-round
summer

SAW ✓ **IT!**

STAN'S COOL STUFF

This bird feeds on the ground, pecking at seeds, and also at tiny grains of rock, which helps it break down food in its stomach. Parents **regurgitate** a liquid, called **crop-milk**, to feed to their young (**squab**) during their first few days of life.

Eurasian Collared-Dove

Look for the black collar on the back of neck

What to look for:
pale gray bird with a slightly darker back, wings and tail, and a black collar on the **nape** of neck; tail is long and squared off at the end

Where you'll find them:
wherever it can scratch for seeds

Calls and songs:
gives a series of coos, often during a **display**

On the move:
usually found in small to large flocks; fast flaps, then glides with wings in a V

What they eat:
seeds and fruit; visits ground and seed feeders

Nest:
platform on a building, balcony, barn or shed, or under a bridge; Mom and Dad construct it

Eggs, chicks and childcare:
3–5 creamy-white eggs; Mom and Dad sit on the eggs and **regurgitate** a liquid food, called **crop-milk**, to feed to the young (**squab**) during their first few days of life

Spends the winter:
doesn't **migrate**; stays in Texas year-round

STAN'S COOL STUFF

This non-native dove is originally from Asia. People brought it into the Bahamas, and then it flew into Florida in the 1980s. Since then it has spread across the country. Scientists believe that this bird will continue to expand its range across more of North America.

Rock Pigeon

Look for the gleaming, iridescent patches

What to look for:

color pattern varies; usually shades of gray with gleaming, **iridescent** patches of green mixed with blue; often has a light rump patch

Size
13"

Where you'll find them:

nearly anyplace where it can scratch for seeds

Nest
PLATFORM

Calls and songs:

a series of coos, usually given during a **display**

On the move:

typically in small to large flocks; flaps rapidly, then glides with wings in a V shape

Feeder
GROUND

What they eat:

seeds and fruit; visits ground and seed feeders

Nest:

platform on a building, balcony, barn or shed, or under a bridge

year-round

Eggs, chicks and childcare:

1–2 white eggs; Mom and Dad sit on the eggs and **regurgitate** a liquid, called **crop-milk**, to feed to the young (**squab**) for their first few days of life

Spends the winter:

doesn't **migrate**; stays in Texas year-round

SAW ✓ **IT!**

STAN'S COOL STUFF

The Rock Pigeon was introduced to North America by early settlers from Europe. Years of breeding in captivity have made it one of the few birds that has a variety of colors. It's also one of the few birds that can drink without tilting its head back.

Willet

Look for the boldly patterned wings

WINTER

BREEDING
pg. 111

What to look for:
gray bird with a white belly, and gray legs and bill; distinctive black-and-white pattern on the wings, seen flashing in flight or during **display**

Where you'll find them:
at the beach

Calls and songs:
calls "pill-will-willet" during the breeding season; gives a "kip-kip-kip" alarm **call** as it takes flight

On the move:
easy to identify due to the black-and-white wing pattern that flashes when the bird flaps rapidly

What they eat:
insects, small fish, small crabs, worms and clams

Nest:
ground nest; Mom builds the nest

Eggs, chicks and childcare:
3–5 olive-colored eggs with dark marks; parents sit on the eggs and feed the young

Spends the winter:
in coastal Texas, other Gulf Coast states and Mexico, Central and South America

Size
14-16"

Nest
GROUND

Feeder
NONE

year-round
migration

SAW ✓ IT!

STAN'S COOL STUFF

This bird is seen along the coast and is very common on beaches all winter. It is a medium-sized sandpiper that uses its long bill to probe into sand in search of food. It nests on the ground along the East and Gulf coasts, in some western states and in Canada.

Canada Goose

Look for the white cheek strap

What to look for:

large gray goose with a black neck and head, and a white chin and cheek strap

Where you'll find them:

wetlands, ponds, lakes, rivers and just about any **habitat** with some water

Calls and songs:

belts out its classic "honk-honk-honk," especially during flight

On the move:

flies in a **flock** in a large V shape when traveling long distances

What they eat:

aquatic plants, insects and seeds

Nest:

ground nest of **vegetation** formed into a mound, usually very near or on water

Eggs, chicks and childcare:

5–10 white eggs; Mom incubates the eggs; young follow the parents around and learn what to eat

Spends the winter:

in Texas and southern states; moves around to find food

Size
25-43"

Nest
GROUND

Feeder
NONE

year-round
winter

SAW IT!

STAN'S COOL STUFF

Males guard the **flock**, bobbing their heads and hissing whenever people approach. Adults **molt** their flight feathers while raising the young, making families temporarily flightless. Canada Geese start to breed in their third year. Adults stay together for many years.

Great Blue Heron

Look for the long yellow bill

What to look for:

tall gray heron with black eyebrows that end in plumes off the back of the head, neck feathers that drop down like a necklace, and a long yellow bill

Where you'll find them:

open water, from small ponds to large lakes

Calls and songs:

when startled, it barks repeatedly like a dog and keeps at it while flying away

On the move:

holds its neck in an S shape in flight and slightly cups its wings, trailing its legs straight out behind

What they eat:

small fish, frogs, insects, snakes and baby birds

Nest:

platform; in a tree near or over open water; in a **colony** of up to 100 birds

Eggs, chicks and childcare:

3–5 blue-green eggs; parents incubate the eggs and feed the **brood**

Spends the winter:

in Texas, other southern states, Mexico, Central and South America

REAL QUICK

Size
42-48"

Nest
PLATFORM

Feeder
NONE

year-round

SAW IT!

STAN'S COOL STUFF

One of the most common herons in Texas. It stalks fish in shallow water and strikes at mice, squirrels and anything else it can capture on land. Red-winged Blackbirds (pg. 25) often attack it to prevent it from taking their babies out of their nests.

177

Sandhill Crane

Look for the red cap

What to look for:

super-tall gray crane with a long neck and legs and a scarlet-red cap; wings and body are often stained rusty-brown

Where you'll find them:

wetlands, small and large

Calls and songs:

a very loud and distinctive rattling **call**, often heard before the bird is seen; call is one of the loudest due to a very long windpipe (**trachea**)

On the move:

wings look like they're flicking in flight, with the upstroke quicker than the downstroke; can fly at great heights of over 10,000 feet

What they eat:

insects, fruit, worms, plants and amphibians

Nest:

ground nest of aquatic plants shaped into a mound

Eggs, chicks and childcare:

2 olive-colored eggs with brown marks; Mom and Dad sit on the eggs; to get fed, babies follow their parents

Spends the winter:

in Texas, other southern states and Mexico

Size
42-48"

Nest
GROUND

Feeder
NONE

migration
winter

SAW IT!

STAN'S COOL STUFF

The Sandhill is one of the tallest birds in the country. Sandhills do a cool mating dance: a pair will first bow, then jump, cackle loudly, flap their wings, and finally, flip sticks and grass into the air.

179

Ruby-throated Hummingbird

Look for the gleaming ruby-red throat

MALE

FEMALE

What to look for:
male is a tiny **iridescent** green bird with a black throat patch that shimmers bright ruby-red in direct sunlight; female lacks the throat patch

Where you'll find them:
many habitats, from yards and parks to forests

Calls and songs:
will chatter or buzz to communicate; doesn't sing or hum a melody—it's the incredibly fast flapping wings that create the humming sound

On the move:
hummingbirds are the only birds that can fly backward; also hovers in midair and flies straight up and straight down!

What they eat:
nectar and insects; visits nectar feeders

Nest:
stretchy cup of plant materials and spiderwebs; glues bits of **lichen** to the outside for camouflage

Eggs, chicks and childcare:
2 white eggs; Mom does all egg and chick care

Spends the winter:
in Texas, other southern states, to Mexico and Central America

Nest
CUP

Feeder
NECTAR

year-round
summer

SAW IT!

STAN'S COOL STUFF

This is the tiniest bird in the state, with approximately the same weight as a U.S. penny. It flaps 50–60 times per second or more in normal flight. It breathes 250 times per minute, and its heart beats up to 1,260 times per minute! It feeds at colorful tube-shaped flowers.

Black-chinned Hummingbird

Look for the violet-blue throat

MALE

FEMALE

What to look for:
male is a tiny iridescent green bird with a black throat patch that looks violet-blue in sunlight; black chin; white chest and belly; female lacks the throat patch and black chin

Where you'll find them:
widespread; scrubby areas, parks and yards

Calls and songs:
does not sing; will chatter or buzz to communicate; the humming sound comes from the incredibly fast flapping of its wings, nearly 80 times per second!

On the move:
can fly backward; zips back and forth

What they eat:
nectar, insects; will come to nectar feeders

Nest:
cup; Mom builds it

Eggs, chicks and childcare:
2 white eggs without marks; Mom sits on the eggs and feeds the young

Spends the winter:
in Texas and Central and South America

REAL QUICK

Size
3³/₄"

Nest
CUP

Feeder
NECTAR

summer
migration
winter

SAW **IT!**

STAN'S COOL STUFF

Weighing only 2-3 grams, a Black-chinned Hummingbird only weighs about as much as a penny! It has a very fast heart rate: 480 beats per minute! Males return to Texas in the spring before females do.

Painted Bunting

Look for the vivid blue head

MALE

FEMALE

What to look for:

male has a vivid blue head, a lime-green back and an orange-to-red chest and belly, with dark wings and tail; female is bright green above, light green below

Where you'll find them:

backyard gardens, brushy roads, thick hedges, woodlands with lots of **vegetation**, scrublands

Calls and songs:

sings loud warbling phrases

On the move:

male flies with exaggerated wing beats, quivers his wings and bows his head to **display** to female

What they eat:

seeds, insects; visits seed feeders in wooded yards

Nest:

cup; made of grass and lined with animal hair; usually in a deep, tangled mass of vines

Eggs, chicks and childcare:

3–5 pale blue eggs with brown marks; Mom sits on the eggs; Mom and Dad feed the babies

Spends the winter:

in Mexico, the Caribbean and Central and South America

Size
5½"

Nest
CUP

Feeder
HOPPER

summer

SAW ● IT!

STAN'S COOL STUFF

No other bird can compare with the striking colors of the male Painted Bunting. The female is also hard to confuse with other birds. Shy, the male and female move around on the ground under a tangle of branches or through leafy growth without being seen.

185

Mallard

Look for the green head

MALE

FEMALE
pg. 123

What to look for:
green head with a white **necklace**, rusty-brown chest, gray sides, yellow bill, orange legs and feet

Where you'll find them:
lakes and ponds, rivers and streams, and maybe even your backyard

Calls and songs:
the male doesn't quack; when you think of how a duck sounds, it's based on the female Mallard's classic loud quack

On the move:
sometimes in huge flocks with hundreds of ducks; mostly in small flocks of 6–10, especially in spring

What they eat:
seeds, aquatic plants and insects; visits ground feeders offering corn

Nest:
ground nest; Mom builds it from plants nearby

Eggs, chicks and childcare:
7–10 greenish-to-whitish eggs; Mom incubates the eggs and leads the young to food

Spends the winter:
in Texas and other southern states

REAL QUICK

Size
19–21"

Nest
GROUND

Feeder
GROUND

year-round
winter

SAW ✓ **IT!**

STAN'S COOL STUFF

This is a dabbling duck, tipping forward in shallow water to eat plants on the bottom. Only the male has black feathers in the center of its tail that curl upward. The name "Mallard" means "male" and refers to the males, which don't help raise their young.

Northern Shoveler

Look for the large, shovel-like bill

MALE

FEMALE
pg. 125

What to look for:
shiny, **iridescent** green head with rusty sides, a white chest and a super-large, spoon-shaped bill

Where you'll find them:
shallow wetlands, ponds and small lakes

Calls and songs:
male gives a crazy-sounding combination of popping and quacking, calling, "puk-puk, puk-puk, puk-puk"; female gives a classic quack **call**

On the move:
swims in tight circles, stirring up insects to eat; small flocks of 5–10 birds swim with bills pointing toward the water; flocks fly in tight formation

What they eat:
enjoys aquatic insects; likes plants, too

Nest:
ground nest; Mom forms plant material into a circle

Eggs, chicks and childcare:
9–12 olive-colored eggs; Mom sits on the eggs and leads her little shovelers to food

Spends the winter:
in Texas and other southern states, the Caribbean, Mexico and Central America

REAL QUICK

Size
19–21"

Nest
GROUND

Feeder
NONE

winter

SAW IT!

STAN'S COOL STUFF

The Northern Shoveler is a medium-sized duck. It is the only shoveler species found in North America. The name "Shoveler" refers to its peculiar, shovel-like bill. It feeds by using its bill to sift tiny aquatic insects and plants floating on the water's surface.

189

Baltimore Oriole

Look for the black head

MALE

FEMALE
pg. 217

What to look for:
flaming orange bird with a black head and back, and black wings with white wing bars

Where you'll find them:
parks, yards and forests; in treetops, where it feeds on caterpillars

Calls and songs:
a fantastic songster, singing loudly; often heard before it is seen

On the move:
often returns to the same area year after year

What they eat:
insects, fruit and **nectar**; comes to nectar, orange-half and grape jelly feeders

Nest:
pendulous; an interesting nest that looks like a sock hanging from an outer branch of a tall tree

Eggs, chicks and childcare:
4–5 bluish eggs with brown marks; Mom sits on the eggs; Mom and Dad do the childcare

Spends the winter:
in Mexico, the Caribbean and Central and South America

REAL QUICK

Size
7-8"

Nest
PENDULOUS

Feeder
NECTAR

summer
migration

SAW IT!

STAN'S COOL STUFF

Orioles visit feeders that offer sugar water (nectar), orange halves or grape jelly. Parents bring their young to feeders. Young males start out looking like females and turn orange and black at 1½ years.

House Finch

Look for the reddish face and the brown cap

MALE

YELLOW MALE

FEMALE
pg. 77

What to look for:
red-to-orange face, throat, chest and rump, and a brown cap

Where you'll find them:
forests, city and suburban areas, around homes, parks and farms

Calls and songs:
male sings a loud, cheerful warbling song

On the move:
moves around in small family units; never travels long distances

What they eat:
seeds, fruit and leaf buds; comes to seed feeders and feeders with a glop of grape jelly

Nest:
cup, but occasionally in a cavity; likes to nest in a hanging flower basket or on a front door wreath

Eggs, chicks and childcare:
4–5 pale blue eggs, lightly marked; Mom sits on the eggs and Dad feeds her while she incubates; Mom and Dad feed the **brood**

Spends the winter:
in Texas; moves around to find food

REAL QUICK

Size
5"

Nest
CUP

Feeder
TUBE OR HOPPER

year-round

SAW IT!

STAN'S COOL STUFF

The House Finch is very social and is found across the country. It can be a common bird at feeders. Unfortunately, it suffers from a fatal eye disease that causes the eyes to crust over. It's rare to see a yellow male; yellow **plumage** may be a result of a poor diet.

Vermilion Flycatcher

Look for the bright red color

MALE

FEMALE
pg. 153

What to look for:

a stunningly beautiful bird with a bright red head, crest, chin, breast and belly; black back, wings and tail, and a thick black line by the eyes; thin black bill

Where you'll find them:

parks and open areas with trees, wetlands, scrub

Calls and songs:

a rapid series of high-pitched calls

On the move:

often seen perched low on a tree, pumping its tail up and down while waiting for a flying insect; it flies out to snatch it, then perches again to eat

What they eat:

insects

Nest:

cup; Mom builds it

Eggs, chicks and childcare:

2–4 white eggs with brown marks; Mom and Dad incubate the eggs and feed the young

Spends the winter:

a few stay in the most southern part of Texas; in Mexico

REAL QUICK

Size
6"

Nest
CUP

Feeder
NONE

summer
winter

SAW IT!

STAN'S COOL STUFF

A beautiful bright red bird, the Vermilion Flycatcher flies after insects or hunts them on the ground. When the male wants to attract a female, he raises its crest, fluffs out his chest feathers, fans his tail and sings a song during a fluttery, funny flight.

Northern Cardinal

Look for the black mask

MALE

FEMALE
pg. 93

What to look for:
all-red bird with a black mask, and a large red crest and bill

Where you'll find them:
wide variety of habitat, including backyards and parks; usually likes thick **vegetation**

Calls and songs:
calls "whata-cheer-cheer-cheer" in spring; both male and female sing and give chip notes all year

On the move:
short flights from **cover** to cover, often landing on the ground

What they eat:
loves sunflower seeds and enjoys insects, fruit, peanuts and **suet**; visits seed feeders

Nest:
cup of twigs and bark strips; often low in a tree

Eggs, chicks and childcare:
3–4 speckled bluish-white eggs; Mom and Dad share the incubating and feeding duties

Spends the winter:
doesn't **migrate**; gathers with other cardinals and moves around to find good sources of food

REAL QUICK

Size
8-9"

Nest
CUP

Feeder
TUBE OR HOPPER

year-round

SAW ✓ IT!

STAN'S COOL STUFF

The Northern Cardinal is one of the few species that has both male and female songsters. Like the females, males sing loud, complex songs. Cardinals are the first to arrive at feeders in the morning and the last to leave before dark.

Redhead

Look for the red head and neck

MALE

FEMALE
pg. 121

What to look for:
bright red head and neck with a black chest and tail; gray sides and back; three-colored bill with a light blue base, a white ring and a black tip

Where you'll find them:
wetlands, ponds, lakes, and rivers

Calls and songs:
a wheezy cat-like meow

On the move:
small flocks in fast flight

What they eat:
seeds, aquatic plants, insects

Nest:
ground, Mom builds usually builds it directly on surface of water, using large mats of vegetation

Eggs, chicks and childcare:
9–14 pale white eggs without marks; Mom incubates the eggs and shows the young what to eat

Spends the winter:
in Texas, near water

REAL QUICK

Size
18-20"

Nest
GROUND

Feeder
NONE

winter

SAW IT!

STAN'S COOL STUFF

Found in large bodies of water, these ducks forage along the shoreline, feeding on seeds, aquatic plants and insects. They also love to eat snails. When the male wants to attract a female, he stretches out his neck as a way to show off.

Roseate Spoonbill

Look for the flat, spoon-shaped bill

JUVENILE

What to look for:
overall pink with red highlights; a white neck with a black patch on the back of the head; a heavy, spoon-shaped flat bill and long red legs; **juvenile** is paler than the adults

Where you'll find them:
freshwater habitats and around the coast

Calls and songs:
usually silent but will make grating grunting sounds when startled or at the nesting **colony**

On the move:
flies in lines with its legs outstretched; walks in shallow water, swinging its bill to sift out fish and aquatic bugs; often in flocks of 30 or more birds

What they eat:
fish, aquatic insects, shrimp, snails, worms, leeches

Nest:
platform; in a mixed colony with herons in trees

Eggs, chicks and childcare:
1–4 olive-colored eggs with dark marks; parents share the **incubation** duties and take turns feeding the kids

Spends the winter:
in Texas; along the coast

REAL QUICK

Size
30-34"

Nest
PLATFORM

Feeder
NONE

year-round
summer

SAW IT!

STAN'S COOL STUFF

The Roseate Spoonbill was devastated in the 1800s from hunters seeking its wing feathers. These were used in women's hats and fans. It's made a comeback, but now **habitat** destruction is limiting its numbers. This unusual pink bird is related to the Ibis (pg. 211).

Laughing Gull
Look for the black head "hood"

BREEDING

WINTER

What to look for:
black head "**hood**" with a white neck, chest and belly; gray wings with black wing tips; orange bill; in winter **plumage** head is gray and white with a black bill

Where to find them:
along the coasts; freshwater and saltwater sites

Calls and songs:
a loud series of calls that sound like laughter; male tosses his head back and calls to attract a mate

On the move:
almost always in groups, moving from one water **habitat** to another

What they eat:
fish, insects on land and in the water

Nest:
ground nest; lined with grass, sticks and rocks; nests in a marsh in a large **colony**

Eggs, chicks and childcare:
2–4 olive-colored eggs with brown marks; parents sit on the eggs and **regurgitate** food to feed the young

Spends the winter:
in coastal Texas

STAN'S COOL STUFF

It takes this gull a few years to get adult plumage. During the first year, the young start out mostly brown and gray. They look like adults during the second year, but they don't have an all-black head "hood." **Juveniles** get the breeding plumage in the third year.

203

Ring-billed Gull
Look for the black ring on the bill

BREEDING

WINTER

What to look for:
white gull with gray wings and a yellow bill with a black ring near the tip; winter **plumage** has speckles on the head and neck

Where you'll find them:
shores of large lakes and rivers; often at garbage dumps and parking lots

Calls and songs:
calls out a wide variety of loud, rising squawks and squeals—classic gull sounds

On the move:
strong flight with constant wing flaps

What they eat:
insects and fish; it also picks through garbage, scavenging for other food

Nest:
ground nest; defends a small area around it

Eggs, chicks and childcare:
2–4 off-white eggs with brown marks; Mom and Dad take turns incubating the eggs and feeding their young

Spends the winter:
in Texas, other southern states and Mexico

STAN'S COOL STUFF

This is one of the most common gulls in the country. Hundreds of these birds often flock together. The ring on the bill appears after the first winter. In the fall of the first three years, the birds have a different plumage. In the third year, they grow adult plumage.

Cattle Egret
Look for the light-orange crest

Content

What to look for:

stocky white bird with a large round head, a light-orange crest, chest and back, and a reddish-orange bill and legs

Where you'll find them:

in pastures, hunting insects at cow and horse manure; attracted to sites of field fires to hunt newly exposed insects and small animals

Calls and songs:

repeats a raspy **call** over and over

On the move:

almost always in small groups of 3–5; in flight, holds its head near its body, bending its neck

What they eat:

insects, small mammals, fish and frogs

Nest:

platform; Mom and Dad build it

Eggs, chicks and childcare:

2–5 light blue-green eggs; Mom and Dad take turns incubating and feeding the young

Spends the winter:

many don't **migrate**; stays in the southern part of Texas year-round, moving around to find food

Mostly White / REAL QUICK / Size 18-22" / Nest PLATFORM / Feeder NONE / year-round summer / SAW IT!

STAN'S COOL STUFF

Originally from Africa, this egret came to South America around 1880, reaching Texas in 1954. To hunt, it wiggles its neck and head back and forth and from side to side, while holding its body still. Then it stabs at **prey** and tosses it to the back of its mouth.

207

Snowy Egret
Look for the bright-yellow feet

What to look for:

all-white egret with a black bill and legs, bright-yellow feet, and long feather plumes on the head, neck and back; yellow patch at the base of the bill

Where you'll find them:

in wetlands and often with other egrets

Calls and songs:

usually silent; when startled, gives a loud, raspy, nasal **call** as it flies away

On the move:

flies with its neck in an S shape and legs trailing

What they eat:

aquatic insects and small fish

Nest:

platform; in a **colony** that may have up to several hundred nests; nests are low in shrubs that are 5–10 feet tall or are on the ground, usually mixed among other egret and heron nests

Eggs, chicks and childcare:

3–5 light blue-green eggs; parents alternate sitting on the eggs and feeding the **hatchlings**

Spends the winter:

in coastal Texas and other Gulf Coast states

STAN'S COOL STUFF

The Snowy Egret was hunted to near extinction in the late 1800s for its long handsome feather plumes. It hunts actively for **prey**, moving around quickly in the water. It uses its feet to stir up small fish and aquatic insects, which it swiftly snaps up to eat.

White Ibis

Look for the long, down-curving bill

BREEDING

JUVENILE

What to look for:

white bird with a long, down-curving orange-to-red bill, pink skin on the face, pink legs, and black wing tips, seen only in flight; **juvenile plumage** is brown-and-white for the first two years

Where you'll find them:

in freshwater and saltwater habitats, but it prefers places with fresh water

Calls and songs:

just makes short grunts at the nesting **colony**

On the move:

flies in groups of 30 or more birds

What they eat:

aquatic bugs, crayfish and other **crustaceans**, fish

Nest:

platform; in a large colony; builds a well-made nest with sticks

Eggs, chicks and childcare:

2–3 light blue eggs with dark marks; Mom and Dad share **incubation** duty and feed the young

Spends the winter:

in coastal Texas and other Gulf Coast states

REAL QUICK

Size
23-27"

Nest
PLATFORM

Feeder
NONE

year-round

SAW IT!

STAN'S COOL STUFF

This bird has been increasing in Texas over the past 50 years, with inland sightings getting more common. It's a year-round resident along the coast. Males are larger than females and have longer bills. Juveniles are brown, unlike the adults.

Great Egret

Look for the long, thin white neck

What to look for:
tall and thin white egret with a long neck, long legs and a long, pointed yellow bill

Where you'll find them:
shallow wetlands, ponds and lakes

Calls and songs:
gives a loud, dry croak if disturbed or when it squabbles for a nest site at the **colony**

On the move:
holds its neck in an S shape during flight; slowly stalks in shallow water, looking for fish to spear with its sharp bill

What they eat:
small fish, aquatic insects, frogs and crayfish

Nest:
platform; in a colony of up to 100 birds

Eggs, chicks and childcare:
2–3 light blue eggs; Mom and Dad sit on the eggs and give food to the **hatchlings**

Spends the winter:
in Texas and other southern states, Mexico and Central America

SAW IT!

STAN'S COOL STUFF

From the 1800s to the early 1900s, the Great Egret was hunted to near extinction for its beautiful long plumes, which were used to decorate women's hats. The plumes grow near the tail during the breeding season. Today, the egret is a protected bird.

American Goldfinch
Look for the black forehead

MALE

FEMALE

WINTER MALE

Mostly Yellow

What to look for:

male is a bright canary-yellow bird with a black forehead, wings and tail; female is olive-yellow and lacks a black forehead; winter male resembles the female

Where you'll find them:

open fields, scrubby areas, woodlands, backyards

Calls and songs:

male sings a pleasant high-pitched song; gives **twitter** calls during flight

On the move:

appears roller coaster-like in flight

What they eat:

loves seeds and insects; comes to seed (especially thistle) feeders

Nest:

cup; builds its nest in late summer and lines the cup with the soft, silky down from wild thistle

Eggs, chicks and childcare:

4–6 pale blue eggs; Mom incubates the eggs and Dad pitches in to help her feed the babies

Spends the winter:

in Texas; flocks of up to 20 birds move around in winter

REAL QUICK

Size
5"

Nest
CUP

Feeder
TUBE OR
HOPPER

winter

SAW IT!

STAN'S COOL STUFF

The American Goldfinch is often called Wild Canary due to its canary-colored **plumage**. This cute little feeder bird is almost always in small flocks, visiting thistle tube feeders that offer Nyjer seed. A late-nesting bird with most nesting in August.

Baltimore Oriole

Look for the gray-brown wings

FEMALE

MALE
pg. 191

What to look for:
pale yellow bird with orange tones and gray-brown wings with white wing bars

Where you'll find them:
parks, yards and forests; in treetops, where it feeds on caterpillars

Calls and songs:
a fantastic songster, singing loudly; often heard before it is seen

On the move:
often returns to the same area year after year

What they eat:
insects, fruit and **nectar**; comes to nectar, orange-half and grape jelly feeders

Nest:
pendulous; an interesting nest that looks like a sock hanging from an outer branch of a tall tree

Eggs, chicks and childcare:
4–5 bluish eggs with brown marks; Mom sits on the eggs; Mom and Dad do the childcare

Spends the winter:
in Mexico, the Caribbean and Central and South America

STAN'S COOL STUFF

Orioles visit feeders that offer sugar water (nectar), orange halves or grape jelly. Parents bring their young to feeders. Young males start out looking like females and turn orange and black at 1½ years.

Eastern & Western Meadowlark
Look for the V-shaped black necklace

EASTERN

WESTERN

What to look for:

a robin-shaped bird with a yellow chest and belly and a V-shaped black **necklace**; white outer tail feathers, usually seen when flying away; short tail

Where to find them:

meadows, open grassy country, roadsides

Calls and songs:

sings a wonderfully clear flute-like whistling song

On the move:

if you move toward it when it's perching on a fence post, it will quickly dive into tall grass

What they eat:

insects and seeds

Nest:

cup; on the ground in dense **cover**; Mom builds the nest by herself

Eggs, chicks and childcare:

3–5 white eggs with brown marks; Mom sits on the eggs, but both parents feed the **hatchlings**

Spends the winter:

in Texas and other southern states, Mexico and Central America

Size
9"

Nest
CUP

Feeder
NONE

Eastern

Western

year-round
migration
winter

SAW IT!

STAN'S COOL STUFF

They are members of the blackbird family, which makes them relatives of orioles and grackles. Like most ground-dwelling birds, their populations have gone down greatly in the last 50 years. A wonderful songster, this bird often runs around before flying.

BIRD FOOD FUN FOR THE FAMILY

If you and your family like to do fun projects together, making your own bird food and bird-feeding items might be just the right ones to try. Chances are good that you already have most of the ingredients at home to make delicious and nutritious treats for your wild bird friends.

You'll be doing these projects in the kitchen, so show your mom or dad the following sections. They're written specifically with the whole family in mind. For example, you may need to check with a parent or guardian for help with such tasks as grocery shopping, stovetop cooking or food preparation, like cutting up fresh fruit.

Starter Snacks and Fruit Treats

You can start by offering some food that's already in your kitchen. Peanut butter attracts a lot of birds! Simply use a spatula to smear some on the bark of a nearby tree where you can watch it from a window. Or use a piece of firewood: prop it up or hang it with a rope and slather it with peanut butter—then watch the birds go wild.

To offer treats like raisins, dates and currants, place them outside in a nonbreakable small bowl with a few holes drilled in the bottom for drainage. Waxwings, robins, catbirds and many other birds love small dried fruit, and some will be flying in shortly to get some.

Putting out fresh fruit, such as apples and oranges, is another great way to attract bright and colorful birds to your yard. Cut these into small, manageable pieces, and offer the snacks on the tray of a feeder.

Another cool way to serve an orange is to cut one in half and place the halves sunny-side up on a feeder or branch. This arrangement allows birds to easily feast on the sweet fruit contained inside the rind. Sometimes it's best to impale the orange half on a nail to stop it from rolling away.

Plain and unsalted nuts, especially peanuts, pecans and walnuts, make wonderful treats for birds. Simply add these to a feeder tray with seeds or place them in a tube feeder for nuts.

Easy Bird Food Recipes

Preparing bird food of any kind shows that you care about the birds in your backyard. Now, are you ready to try making some recipes? Below are just a few suggestions. You can find much more online.

Sweet Homemade Nectar

Nectar is a superb food for many birds. Studies of nectar from flowers have shown that the average flower nectar is 25 percent sucrose. Sucrose is a simple sugar, so to make the correct strength of homemade nectar (sugar water), mix a ratio of 1 part sugar to 4 parts water. You'll discover that hummingbirds, orioles and woodpeckers will thoroughly enjoy the sweet drink that you made.

INGREDIENTS
¼ cup granulated white sugar
1 cup warm water

DIRECTIONS: Add the sugar to the water and stir to dissolve. If you prefer, you can boil the water first so the sugar dissolves more quickly. Cool to room temperature before filling your feeder. Store any extra in the refrigerator or freezer.

NOTES: Never substitute brown sugar or honey for white sugar. Also, there is no need to add red food coloring because the birds will be attracted to any amount of red on any part of your **nectar** feeder.

Birds-Go-Wild Spread

INGREDIENTS
½ cup raisins
½ cup granola
½ cup oatmeal
½ cup Cheerios
16-ounce jar smooth peanut butter

DIRECTIONS: Mix dry ingredients in a large mixing bowl. Warm the peanut butter in a microwave or place the jar in warm water to soften. Scoop out the softened peanut butter, and mix well with dry ingredients until smooth.

Spread on tree bark or smear a few dollops on the tray of a feeder.

Love-It-Nutty Butter

INGREDIENTS
2 cups shelled peanuts, unsalted
2 cups shelled walnuts, unsalted
¼ cup raisins
3–5 tablespoons coconut oil or other vegetable oil

DIRECTIONS: Toss dry ingredients into a food processor. Start blending. Add oil until the mixture reaches a smooth, thick consistency. Store in refrigerator.

Smear on a wooden board with grooves or spread on tree bark.

Make Your Own Suet

You and your family can make outstanding **suet** recipes at home, too. Suet is animal fat, often from cows, and there are several convenient ways to get it for your recipes.

A quick way is to purchase plain suet cakes. In store-bought suet, the fat has already been melted down (**rendered**). A cheaper way might be to buy fat trimmings in bulk from your local butcher or large amounts of **lard** at your grocery store. A clever way to get rendered fat from your own kitchen is for an adult to pour fat drippings from cooked bacon, pork and beef into an empty, clean can. When the fat has cooled and solidified, cover and refrigerate to save for future use.

Easy-Peasy Suet

INGREDIENTS
1 cup solidified fat of your choice
1 cup chunky peanut butter
3 cups ground cornmeal
1 cup white flour
1 cup black oil sunflower seeds or peanuts

DIRECTIONS: In a large pot, melt the fat over low heat. Do not heat quickly or the fat might burn. Strain the fat through a **cheesecloth** to remove any chunks, and then pour the liquid back into the pot.

Add the peanut butter to the fat. Stir over low heat until the mixture melts and consistency is smooth. Remove from heat. Add the cornmeal and flour, and mix until stiff. Add the sunflower seeds or peanuts, and mix thoroughly.

Pour into a mold or container. With a spatula, spread out the mixture and smooth the top. Cool completely, then cut into squares. Store in freezer.

Simply Super Suet

INGREDIENTS
2 cups **suet** or **lard**
1 cup peanut butter
2 cups yellow cornmeal
2 cups cracked corn
1 cup black oil sunflower seeds

DIRECTIONS: In a large pot, melt the suet or lard over low heat. Add the peanut butter, stirring until melted and well mixed. Add remaining ingredients, and mix.

Pour into baking pans or forms and allow to cool. Cut into chunks or shapes. Store in freezer.

Yummy Bird-Feeding Projects

Bird-feeding projects are super activities for families, and they can be a big hit at special occasions, such as birthday parties. These very attractive ornaments and feeders also make unique gifts for the holidays and family celebrations.

Birdseed Ornaments

INGREDIENTS
cookie cutters in any shape
nonstick cooking spray
½ cup water
3 tablespoons white corn syrup
2½ teaspoons unflavored gelatin
¾ cup white flour
4 cups black oil sunflower seeds
10- to 12-inch pieces of string or **jute** twine

DIRECTIONS: Place the cookie cutters on wax paper and spray with nonstick cooking spray. Set aside.

In a saucepan, bring the water and corn syrup to a boil. Reduce heat and stir in gelatin until completely mixed. Do not overcook.

Transfer the hot liquid to a bowl. Add the flour, and mix until smooth. Add the sunflower seeds, and mix well. Mixture will now be thick.

Use a spatula to fill each cookie cutter. Be sure to press the seeds into all parts of the shapes. Roll any extra mixture into balls. Poke one hole through each shape and each ball with a pencil or similar object.

When cooled, pop out the ornaments from the cookie cutters. Thread a length of string or twine through each hole, and tie the ends to form a loop. Loop each of your ornaments over nearby branches, and watch the birds come to feast!

Pine Cone Birdseed Feeders

Try your hand at making this fabulous little bird feeder from an ordinary pine cone. It's fun and easy, and everyone in your family can make their own.

INGREDIENTS (per person)
1 pine cone
10- to 12-inch piece of string or **jute** twine
peanut butter
birdseed

DIRECTIONS: Tie a piece of string or twine to a pine cone. Roll the cone in peanut butter, filling the spaces between the "petals" (bracts) and coating the entire surface. Then roll the cone in birdseed until the seeds completely cover the peanut butter.

Hang the feeder outside where you can see the birds feeding on it, and enjoy the show!

MORE ACTIVITIES FOR THE BIRD-MINDED

Nothing brings family and friends closer together than a shared interest. Birding and backyard bird feeding are enjoyable, year-round activities that many find appealing. Here are some things to do that are not only fun for everyone but also supportive for the birds.

Help Birds Build Their Nests

A thoughtful way for the entire family to work together with birds during spring is to put out a variety of soft and flexible natural items to help birds build their nests.

First, gather some everyday materials around your home that birds will use. Here are some excellent items to offer:

- Yarn, cut into 6-inch-long pieces
- Fabric from an old, clean T-shirt, cut into 6-inch-long strips
- Cotton batting (used for handicrafts)
- Fuzzy pet hair from a brush

Next, place your materials into an unused, clean suet cage. Be sure to let the ends of the yarn and fabric strips hang out, and don't pack the material in tightly. The birds need to be able to take out the items easily.

Hang the cage by a short chain from a tree in early spring, when the birds are starting to construct their nests. And then, wait...

Soon, birds will be flying back and forth to the materials and choosing their favorites. It's a delight to see birds making use of your nesting contributions. Not only have you assisted the bird parents, but you've also helped them provide a comfy home for their families. Good job!

Make a Bird-watching List

Making a watch list on **poster board** of the birds that have visited your yard is a handicraft project that the whole family will enjoy. You can decorate the poster any way you like, but it's awesome to show pictures of the birds you've spotted and write notes about the sightings.

Each time you see a new species in your yard, mark it on the poster with the date and time of day. Attach it to the refrigerator, or put it in another prominent place where it's easy for everyone in the family to see and add their updates.

Your watch list is also a valuable way to track the arrival of the first hummingbirds and orioles in your area each spring. If you create a new watch list each year, it could reveal trends in the arrival dates. This information would be of interest not only to your family and friends, but also to your teachers and local birding organizations.

Save the Birds with Hawk Cutouts

Another fun and important project is to make hawk cutouts to attach to your windows. These items will help prevent birds from flying into sheets of glass at your home.

In-flight window strikes are one of the major killers of our wild bird friends. Window reflections of the sky, trees and other natural features in your yard create the illusion to birds that the flight path is clear. When birds see forms of predator birds in the reflections, they will turn away and take another route.

Various web pages show outlines (**silhouettes**) of hawks that you can print and cut out. Check the possibilities, and then pick your favorites.

Tape the cutouts to any large picture windows, as well as other windows and doors with clear glass. This preventive action will greatly reduce the risk of birds crashing headfirst into glass. Then give yourself a high five for helping to save them.

Build Your Very Own Birdhouse

A first-rate project for kids and adults to do together is to construct a birdhouse. Building plans are available online for different kinds of birdhouses for different kinds of birds. Give them a once-over, and pick one that you like best for the birds you want nesting nearby.

The instructions online will help you select the right kind of wood and show you how to cut it to the right sizes. Most importantly, the plans will provide the correct size of the entrance hole for the bird, along with how-to instructions for making it. Most birdhouse projects require hand and power tools, so be sure to work with an adult.

You might even want to make multiple birdhouses with your extended family or your neighbors. With everyone doing different tasks, your team can turn out a bluebird box, a wren box, a robin platform and more!

Create a Bird-Friendly Yard

There is no better way to support the birds in your area than to plant bird-friendly flowers, bushes and trees. There are many varieties of these plants, making it easy to choose some that will be ideal for your yard.

Planting perennials that bloom large and showy flowers each year is an outstanding way to feed hummingbirds. Many shrubs produce attractive **nectar**-filled flowers and then, later in the summer, edible fruit, which the birds love. Numerous tree species offer berries and nuts—foods the birds depend on in late fall.

A yard with grass alone just isn't a friendly **habitat** for birds, so sit down with your family and think about putting in a flower garden or adorning your yard with some shrubs and trees. Soon afterward, you'll be hearing the sweet chirping of birds and a rich repertoire of **birdsong** all around you.

Take a Birding Trip

Everyone loves a good time! For a fun family outing, plan a birding trip to a local park, state park or national wildlife refuge. In spring, you'll be rewarded with migrating warblers. During summer, all of the nesting birds will be feeding babies. In fall, waterfowl will be super-active. Even in winter, there are many amazing birds to see.

Your local nature center is another good place to see birds. Oftentimes nature centers have bird feeders set up to attract birds. Stop in after school or early on Saturday mornings to see what comes to the feeders.

The shores along the Atlantic Ocean and the Gulf of Mexico are fantastic places where other incredible birds gather. Pack a picnic lunch and head out with your family to enjoy both the outdoors and the birds that don't hang around feeders. Cormorants, ospreys and gulls are just some of the cool birds that spend their time around the water.

Practice Good Birding

Finding a stray feather or an empty bird nest is exciting when you and your family are sharing time in nature. Examining these wonders and making a sketch or taking photos are always fun educational opportunities. However, everyone should be aware that collecting, possessing or owning wild bird feathers, nests, and even bird eggs is not permitted under federal law.

It may seem silly that a lost feather or vacant bird nest needs protecting, but very important laws stop people from buying, selling and trading these items. In the past, a lively market for feathers, bird nests, and also eggs led to widespread killing of birds, some to near extinction. To prevent from this happening again, strong laws were passed to safeguard all of our bird species.

So enjoy seeing, studying and learning about birds, but please don't take any feathers, nests or eggs with you out of their natural environment. Leave them just as you found them, and perhaps someone else will also get the opportunity to benefit from studying them.

CITIZEN SCIENCE PROJECTS

I can't think of a more exciting way to learn about birds and expand the birding experience than to take part in a citizen science project. If you are unfamiliar with citizen science projects, they are sponsored by organizations in which citizens like yourself can contribute in a meaningful way to actual scientific projects right from your own home! Most projects don't take much time and can be fun family activities, with everyone sharing what they learned about birds.

There are simple citizen science projects that might have you just count the birds that come to your feeders. Others are more complex and involve more time, effort and perhaps a little traveling. Either way, I'm sure you can find an enjoyable and educational citizen project that will be a perfect fit for your family. Give it a try!

Here are some popular projects and resources for you to explore:

The very well-known Christmas Bird Count winter census, FeederWatch and more

www.birds.cornell.edu/home

Hummingbird migration

https://journeynorth.org/tm/humm/AboutSpring.html

Finding and counting nesting birds

https://nestwatch.org

General citizen science projects for counting birds

www.birdwatchingdaily.com/featured-stories/year-round-citizen-science-projects/

American Kestrel nesting and population study

https://kestrel.peregrinefund.org

LEARNING ABOUT BIRDING ON THE INTERNET

Birding online is another fine way to discover more information about birds—plus it's a terrific way to spend time during rainy summer days and winter evenings after sunset. So check out the websites below, and be sure to share with your family and friends the fabulous things you've learned about birds.

eBird

https://ebird.org/home

American Birding Association: Young Birders

https://www.aba.org/aba-young-birders/

Cornell Lab of Ornithology

www.birds.cornell.edu/home

Author Stan Tekiela's website

www.naturesmart.com

In addition, online birding groups can be of valuable assistance to you as well. Facebook has many pages dedicated to specific areas of the state and the birds that live there. These sites are an excellent, real-time resource that will help you spot birds in your region. Consider joining a Facebook birding group.

GLOSSARY

birdsong: A series of musical notes that a bird strings together in a pleasing melody. Also called a song.

brood: A family of bird brothers and sisters that hatched at around the same time.

brood parasites: Birds that don't nest, incubate or raise families, such as Brown-headed Cowbirds (pg. 19). See *host*.

call: A nonmusical sound, often a single note, that is repeated.

carrion: A dead and often rotting animal's body, or carcass, that is an important food for many other animals, including birds.

cheesecloth: A loosely woven cotton cloth that is used primarily to wrap cheese. It is also used to strain particles from liquids.

colony: A group of birds nesting together in the same area. The size of a colony can range from two pairs to hundreds of birds.

coniferous: A tree or shrub that has evergreen, needle-like leaves and that produces cones.

cotton batting: A light, soft cotton material, often used to stuff quilts.

cover: A dense area of trees or shrubs where birds nest or hide.

crop-milk: A liquid that pigeons and doves regurgitate (spit up) to feed their young.

crustaceans: A large, mainly aquatic group of critters, such as crayfish, crabs and shrimp.

deciduous: A tree or shrub that sheds its leaves every year.

display: An attention-getting behavior of birds to impress and attract a mate, or to draw predators away from the nest. A display may include dramatic movements in flight or on the ground.

double-scratch: A quick double hop that some birds use to find food.

epaulets: Decorative color patches on the shoulders of a bird, as seen in male Red-winged Blackbirds (pg. 25).

excavate: To dig or carefully remove wood or dirt, creating a cavity, hole or tunnel.

fledge: The process of developing flight feathers and leaving the nest.

flock: A group of the same bird species or a gathering of mixed species of birds. Flocks range from a pair of birds to upwards of 10,000 individuals.

habitat: The natural home or environment of a bird.

hatchlings: Baby birds that have recently emerged from their eggs. See *nestlings*.

hood: The markings on the head of a bird, resembling a hood.

horns: A tuft or collection of feathers, usually on top of a bird's head, resembling horns.

host: A bird species that takes care of the eggs and babies of other bird species. See *brood parasites*.

incubation: The process of sitting on bird eggs in the nest to keep them warm until they hatch.

iridescent: A luminous, or bright, quality of feathers, with colors seeming to change when viewed from different angles.

jute: A string of rough fibers made from plants.

juvenile: A bird that isn't an adult yet.

lard: Fat from a pig.

lichen: A unique partnership of plant life and fungi growing together and looking and acting as one organism.

lore: The area on each side of a bird's face between the eye and the base of the bill.

migrate: The regular, predictable pattern of seasonal movement by some birds from one region to another, especially to escape winter.

mollusks: Soft-bodied critters that lack a backbone (invertebrate), such as snails, slugs, clams, oysters and mussels.

molt: The process of dropping old, worn-out feathers and replacing them with new feathers, usually only one feather at a time.

morph: A bird with a color variation. Morphs also sometimes occur in mammals, reptiles, amphibians and insects.

mute: The inability to make or produce audible sounds. The Turkey Vulture (pg. 39), for example, is mostly mute.

nape: The back of a bird's neck.

necklace: The markings around the neck of a bird, as seen in the Eastern Meadowlark (pg. 219).

nectar: A sugar and water solution found in plant flowers.

nestlings: Young birds that have not yet left the nest. See *hatchlings*.

oak savanna: A grassy habitat with scattered oak trees.

pair bond: The relationship between a male and female bird during the mating season.

plumage: The collective set of feathers on a bird at any given time.

poster board: A stiff cardboard that is used for displaying information.

prey: Any critter that is hunted and killed by another for food.

raptor: A flesh-eating bird of prey that hunts and kills for food. Hawks, eagles, ospreys, falcons, owls and vultures are raptors. See *prey*.

refraction: The bending of light.

regurgitate: The process of bringing swallowed food up again to the mouth to feed young birds.

rendered: Animal fat that has been reduced or melted down by heating and then strained in order to make it pure.

sap: The watery liquid that moves up and down within the circulatory system of a tree, carrying nutrients throughout.

silhouettes: Dark shapes or outlines against a lighter background.

speculum: A patch of bright feathers on some birds, such as ducks, found on the wings.

squab: A young pigeon or dove, usually still in the nest. See *nestlings*.

suet: Animal fat, usually beef, that has been heated and made into cakes to feed birds. See *rendered*.

thermals: A column of upward-moving warm air caused by the sun warming the earth. Raptors and other birds gain altitude during flight by "riding" on thermals.

trachea: A large tubelike organ that allows air to pass between the lung and the mouth of a bird. Also called a windpipe.

trill: A fluttering or repeated series of similar-sounding musical notes given by some birds.

twitter: A high-pitched call of a bird. See *call*.

ultraviolet light: A kind of light that is visible to birds and insects but unseen by people.

vegetation: Any plants, especially those found growing in a particular habitat.

warble: A quiet bird song with many different sounds.

waterfowl: A group of similar birds with a strong connection to water. Ducks, geese, and others, including American Coots (pg. 29), are examples of waterfowl.

CHECKLIST/INDEX BY SPECIES

Use the circles to checkmark the birds you've seen.

ABOUT THE AUTHOR

Naturalist, wildlife photographer and writer Stan Tekiela is the originator of the popular state-specific field guide series that includes *Birds of Texas Field Guide*. He has authored more than 195 field guides, nature books, children's books, wildlife audio CDs and playing cards, presenting many species of birds, mammals, reptiles, amphibians, trees, wildflowers and cacti in the United States.

With a Bachelor of Science degree in Natural History from the University of Minnesota and as an active professional naturalist for more than 30 years, Stan studies and photographs wildlife throughout the United States and Canada. He has received various national and regional awards for his books and photographs. Also a well-known columnist and radio personality, his syndicated column appears in more than 25 newspapers, and his wildlife programs are broadcast on a number of Midwest radio stations. Stan can be followed on Facebook and Twitter. He can be contacted via www.naturesmart.com.